D1476167

SOCIAL WORKER EMPOWERMENT
IN
CHILD PROTECTION COURT

ABOUT THE AUTHOR

As a family lawyer, Barry Friesen has represented social workers in child protection cases for ten years and presented court skills training workshops for social workers since 1981. He is also a Gestalt therapist.

SOCIAL WORKER EMPOWERMENT IN CHILD PROTECTION COURT

By

BARRY FRIESEN, B.A., LL.B.

HV
40.8
. U6
F75
1990
West

C H A R L E S C T H O M A S • P U B L I S H E R
Springfield • Illinois • U.S.A.

Published and Distributed Throughout the World by

CHARLES C THOMAS • PUBLISHER
2600 South First Street
Springfield, Illinois 62794-9265

This book is protected by copyright. No part of
it may be reproduced in any manner without
written permission from the publisher.

© *1990 by* CHARLES C THOMAS • PUBLISHER

ISBN 0-398-05690-0

Library of Congress Catalog Card Number: 90-10841

With THOMAS BOOKS *careful attention is given to all details of manufacturing
and design. It is the Publisher's desire to present books that are satisfactory as to their
physical qualities and artistic possibilities and appropriate for their particular use.*
THOMAS BOOKS *will be true to those laws of quality that assure a good name
and good will.*

Printed in the United States of America
SC-R-3

Library of Congress Cataloging-in-Publication Data

Friesen, Barry.
    Social worker empowerment in child protection court / by Barry
Friesen.
        p. cm.
    ISBN 0-398-05690-0
    1. Social workers—United States.   2. Child abuse—United States.
    3. Social workers—Legal status, laws, etc.—United States.
    4. Child abuse—Law and legislation—United States.   I. Title.
HV40.8.U6F75   1990
362.7'68—dc20
                                                                        90-10841
                                                                          CIP

*To Erzsi, my best friend, who taught me the power of love,
and to our three sons, Brin, Troy, and Attila,
who taught me the power of joy.*

PREFACE

The material presented here draws on my experience as a child protection lawyer representing social workers in family court. Many of the approaches and techniques, however, come from court skills workshops I have given to social workers over the past nine years, as well as from my practice as a Gestalt therapist. For me, working with social workers has always been a genuine pleasure. I am indebted to my friends in the social work field for their willingness to share their terrors about the witness stand and about the court process in general, as this has enabled me to appreciate the problems presented by the adversarial legal system from the social worker perspective.

Much has been written about child abuse and neglect. Most of the writing has been directed to social workers in the field. To my knowledge, little has been written to assist social workers in family court, where the ultimate decisions about child abuse and neglect are made. This book is for those who seek a bridge of understanding to the court work side of the child protection field.

I am indebted to Delma Hemming, Joanne Sawadsky, Carole Wood, and Linda Hayes-Newington of the British Columbia Ministry of Social Services for their support of my work, and for their enthusiasm for the exercises and concepts which empower social workers in the court process. I also acknowledge my indebtedness to Linda Galloway and all the members of her Gestalt Discovery Group, from whom I have learned much about the power of personal choice. They have freely offered their insight and their inspiration, and I have accepted both greedily.

The sections discussing games and power plays in court owe a great deal to the pioneering work in transactional analysis by Eric Berne and Claude Steiner, whose ideas I have gratefully adapted.

Child abuse and neglect snap the spine of human understanding. The world owes a great debt to the dedicated individuals who devote themselves to protecting children from risk. Yet when a social worker intervenes to protect a child, she assumes a responsibility fraught with obstacles and little appreciation. This book offers choices about how to transcend the burdens and fears of court process, in hopes of making the witness stand a place of comfort and confidence. I present these choices to social workers everywhere, for kids everywhere, in appreciation.

INTRODUCTION

S ocial workers tend to drop their toolbag of skills on the courthouse
steps. The legal system seems to operate according to secret, incom-
prehensible rules. Members of the helping professions find little comfort
in a court of law, and much aggravation. Court process appears mysterious and unpleasant. The temptation is to give in to the angst, and hope
someone will offer rescue.

No one will.

But no one needs to, because rescue is unnecessary. The places where
angst occurs are rich with personal choice, even though the adversarial
legal system masks the choices available. The legal system offers constant
invitations to social workers to give away their power. It places obstacles
along the road to making the abused or neglected child's life real in the
mind and heart of the family court judge. It insists on a linear, analytical
approach to human relationships, which is foreign and frustrating to
many social workers.

The premise of this book is that social workers are fully empowered to
deal effectively with the intimidating parts of the adversarial legal system.
It is a matter of understanding the dynamics at work and discovering
how to reclaim the power of choice in the places where the win-win belief
system of the helping professions collides with the win-lose belief system
of the players in court.

In conducting court skills training workshops for social workers for
many years, it has been my experience that child protection workers tend
to feel powerless and intimidated in the face of the court system.
Reclaiming that power is not, ultimately, a difficult task. The process
involves choosing to release oneself from the myths and fantasies that
have built up around the legal system and its players, choosing to meet
the legal system on its own terms, and choosing to transform existing
social worker skills to meet the demands of the witness stand. Whether
hostile cross-examination is stressful or easeful is not up to the lawyer
conducting the cross-examination. It is up to the social worker herself,

through choices that remain invisible until they are seen. In this book I have attempted to expose some of the choices available to empower the protection social worker throughout the court process.

I have discussed the basic legal components of protection statutes, but this is not primarily a work about the technical details of legal procedure. The focus is on the dynamics of the processes involved, from the initial intervention to remove a child, to the first appearance in family court, and through to the conclusion of a contested hearing.

Increasingly, social workers have come under attack for the way in which they exercise their discretion to intervene and remove a child at risk. The decision to intervene is not always articulated by social workers in terms the legal system can understand, but I am unable to share the general concern. Ten years of working with them has convinced me that although social workers make easy targets, the real problem is not social worker discretion, but the fact that as a society, legislatively and otherwise, we have barely begun to confront what we are doing to so many of our children. Until we do, I believe we are well-served by the principle that social workers have the right to remove children when they consider them at risk, period. I therefore proceed on this assumption in what follows, and leave criticism of social workers to those who see them differently.

A final note about the choice of gender in the writing that follows. To avoid the disruption of "his/her" throughout the text, I refer to the child before the court, the agency counsel, and the family court judge, in the masculine throughout. The social worker and all other players in the protection process are referred to in the feminine. This choice is arbitrary and for convenience only; I mean no offence to the great numbers of male social workers and female judges and counsel.

CONTENTS

Page

Preface vii

Introduction ix

Chapter

1. SOCIAL WORKERS AND THE LEGAL SYSTEM:
   STEREOTYPES AND MYTHS 3

   The Case of Baby Joseph 3

   The Scapegoat Syndrome In Daily Operation 5

   The Shark Lawyers 6

   The Big Daddy Judge 8

   The Intimidating Courtroom 10

   The Lottery Justice System 11

   The Hopeless Parent 13

   The Steamrollered Child 14

   The Oversensitive Social Worker 15

   Beyond the Scapegoat Syndrome 17

2. PROTECTING KIDS:
   HELP WANTED, HELP UNWANTED 21

   Cliches about Caring for Kids 21

   Kids as Property 23

   Let the Social Workers Take Care of It
   as Long as They Don't Do Anything 26

   Covert Coercion 28

   Media Thirst for Fashionable Cases 30

   Keeping the Faith 31

3. TRIALS AND TRIBULATIONS:
   TAKING THE CASE TO COURT 33

   Removal of the Child for Serious Cause 33

   Dry Runs Before Court 37

Double Bind: Trust Betrayed 40

Rescuer and Persecutor 41

Court: New Game, New Rules 45

Leaving Your Toolbag on the Courthouse Steps 50

4. SELF–ASSESSMENT: COURT SKILLS, COURT HABITS 53

Awareness and Ability 53

State and Parent: the Power Differential 58

Power Plays Before Court 60

Power Plays In Court 63

Court Habits for Every Case 66

Transforming the Social Worker Toolbag 70

Power Parity 82

"Do You Have Any Children of Your Own?" 82

5. PROTECTION STATUTES: AN OVERVIEW 75

The State as a Silver Cloud 75

Judicial and Social Ambivalence 77

Interim Custody 78

Serving Notices 79

The Two-Step Protection Hearing 80

The Mandate to Return the Child 83

Visitation and Expectations 84

6. TRUTH: THE MISTRESS OF MANY FACES 87

The Separate Reality of Court 87

Intuition on the Witness Stand 89

Rumor, Gossip, and Scurrilous Innuendo 90

Self-Fulfilling Prophesies 91

Provable Facts: the Yellow Highlighter Test 92

Types of Evidence 95

Expert Evidence: Hard Science and Soft Science 98

7. COURT: THE BUCK STOPS HERE .103

Discretion and Accountability 103

Honoring Solomon 104

The Judicial Skeptic 105

The Other Players in Court 107

Who Needs Lawyers? 108

Why Court at All: Policy and Politics 109

8. IN THE TRENCHES:
ASSESSING THE STRENGTH OF YOUR CASE 111
  Nailing Down the Issues 111
  Nailing Down the Facts 114
  Brief to Counsel 116
  The Burden of Proof 121
  Bringing the Child's Reality to Court 122
  Conferencing the Case 123
  Consulting your Counsel 124
  Handling of Experts 126
  Coping with Flux 127

9. BEFORE COURT:
HAT TRICKS, ZERO-SUM GAMES, WIN-WIN 129
  Scapegoating in Action 129
  Enemies and Allies 130
  Sharing the Evidence 131
  Transcending the Adversarial System 132
  Inventing Solutions 134
  Letters of Expectation 135
  Statements of Agreed Upon Facts 137
  Arming Opposing Counsel 139
  Co-opting the Court 141

10. IN COURT: SOCIAL WORKER ON TRIAL 143
  Examination-in-Chief 143
  Cross-Examination 147
  The Permeable Boundary 147
  Honoring the Process 148
  Speaking the Case 149
  Resisting Intimidation 150
  Managing Eye Contact 150
  Keeping the Focus on the Child 151
  Giving Credit Where Due 152
  Conceding Error 152
  Claiming Time and Space 153
  Rehearsal and Testing the Waters 153
  Empowering Fantasies 154

Reacting and Responding 155

Maintaining Your Warm 156

11. AFTER COURT: THE POSTMORTEM 157

Coming to Terms with Defeat 157

Coming to Terms with Success 159

Adding to the Toolbag 160

Considering an Appeal 161

Debriefing with Counsel 162

12. LEGAL NOTIONS: SHAKY FOUNDATIONS 165

The Division of Power: Parents, State, Court 165

Law as a "Living Tree" 166

Statutes, Precedents, and Adjective Law 166

The Court's Struggle with Protection Cases 168

Reasons for Judgment 170

The Hearsay Rule in Protection Cases 175

13. JOURNEY TO PROTECTION:
HELPING YOURSELF, HELPING THE CASE,
HELPING THE CHILD 179

Meeting Your Own Needs 179

Limitations of the Job 183

Becoming an Asset to the Case 183

Owning Your Power, Sharing Your Power, Giving It Away 185

Acceptance and Forgiveness 186

Either-Or 187

Love in Process 187

Index 189

SOCIAL WORKER EMPOWERMENT
IN
CHILD PROTECTION COURT

Chapter 1

SOCIAL WORKERS AND THE LEGAL SYSTEM:
STEREOTYPES AND MYTHS

THE CASE OF BABY JOSEPH

In the last four months Baby Joseph has been in and out of the hospital four times. When he is in the hospital, he gains weight. When he is home, his weight falls. Mom says he refuses to eat, or throws up.

Mom and you are no longer pals. She won't agree to Baby Joe going into a special care foster home, as recommended by the medical team. "The doctors are quacks," she says.

You want an hour with your supervisor, but she has meetings scheduled all week. You catch her for five minutes in the hallway. The decision is made to apprehend Baby Joe.

So off to court you go.

Going to court makes you nervous. You invite two of the older workers in your office for coffee to talk about your case. One agrees, but is called away on an emergency case of her own. The other just can't make it. Both wish you luck.

You play telephone tag with your lawyer until just before the switchboard shuts down at 4:30. You tell him it is a "failure to thrive" case. He asks you to explain the syndrome. You fumble through the medical reports, babbling. "I need some conference time," you say.

He is too pressed. "We'll just have to wing it," he says. "Don't worry, you'll do fine." He hangs up and you stare at the phone.

The next morning Mom and Dad are sitting in the court waiting room, looking confident. A well-dressed young woman sits beside them, her attache case on her lap, obviously their lawyer. You approach the parents to say hello, to make contact. Mom refuses to say anything. Dad looks away. The lawyer looks up from her papers. "Is this the social worker?" she asks the Mom. The Mom nods grimly. The lawyer looks you in the eye. You have seen the look before. You are the enemy. "I'd prefer that you stay away from my clients," she says with a tight smile.

3

"You understand." She turns back to her papers. You have been dismissed. You understand, all right. This will be no fun at all.

The case is called. The court clerk is impatient; the list is long this morning. In a few minutes you are called to the witness stand, take the oath, remain standing. The judge tells you sharply to sit down when you testify. You find yourself blushing. You have forgotten this is the short judge, installed behind the bench on a large cushion. He likes witnesses to be seated. Stand up, sit down. Simon says.

The opposing lawyer smiles sweetly at you, her eyes glittering. You have the impression that she has not been fed recently.

Your lawyer asks you questions about the case, but he is having trouble remembering the details you discussed briefly the day before. He sounds irritated, as if he expects you to carry the case on your own.

You fumble with your opening statements. Your mouth is dry and your voice rises half an octave. You are certain that your heartbeat is audible all the way to the back of the courtroom. You make a mistake about the baby's birth date.

The opposing lawyer catches it. "Excuse me, Your Honor, the papers filed indicate December as the birth month. Apparently this worker has made an error." One of many, her voice implies.

Your lawyer is not pleased. "Can you tell the court about the baby's fractures?" he asks.

You are confused. He has asked you a question about the next case on the list, not yours. How should you reply? There is a salty taste on your lips; you have begun to sweat. "This baby has no fractures," you say. "He hasn't gained weight."

Now your lawyer looks confused. He was sure there were fractures. He fluffs in his files, checks the docket, reorients himself.

The two of you struggle through your testimony.

The judge has started to draw pictures of sailboats.

When it is the parents' turn to cross-examine, their lawyer asks, "Exactly how long have you been a social worker?" Your heart sinks.

Eventually you have reluctantly admitted that you have no children of your own, that you have not completely finished college, that the parents *did* bring the baby to the hospital in the first place, and that they have two other apparently normal children. The judge makes his decision.

He feels that the parents have acted responsibly and he is sure that, with your continuing offers of help, the parents will do all right with Baby Joseph. "Certainly there is no evidence of abuse," he says.

You have lost the case. Baby Joseph returns home the next day. You discuss an appeal with your lawyer. "No grounds," he says. "The judge believes in the parents."

Enter the scapegoat syndrome. When the result in a case is not what was expected or desired, there is a need to attribute the cause of it all to something. Myths and stereotypes about the elements of the legal system serve nicely as convenient places to lay the blame. *The myths operate to make the roles of people and systems appear larger and more powerful than they really are. The stereotypes operate to make them appear smaller and less powerful than they really are.*

There is an epic quality to fighting things out in a court of law. The risk presented in the example of Baby Joseph is fundamental: he may starve to death in the hands of his parents. The more severe the consequences to the child, the more likely it is that you may be tempted to give away power to the myths about legal process. It is not a question of resisting the temptation, but removing it. This, in turn, is a matter of becoming *aware* of how the myths work. To do this, let's take a closer look at the myths and stereotypes offered for sale and purchase by the legal system.

The reality is that working to protect the two million kids per year reported neglected or abused (U.S., 1987) can seem to be the loneliest, most unappreciated task in the world. Do other social workers feel this way? The answer is *yes*, certainly at times.

Is there anything *you* can do to make going to court less of a burden? The answer is *yes*.

THE SCAPEGOAT SYNDROME IN DAILY OPERATION

The preceding account of the Baby Joseph case is bleak and unpleasant.

But cases like this one have happened, are happening, and continue to happen in family courts everywhere. Every social worker has cases where the legal system seems to be more enemy than ally.

In fairness, kids *are* successfully protected much of the time. Even so, the court process makes every worker feel occasionally that she is on trial herself, that she is under personal attack on the witness stand.

Why should this be?

The starting point to find the answer is to examine the power given over to the legal system's built-in myths and stereotypes. It is vital to understand how the legal system *actually* works. The myths and stereotypes just get in the way. So let's dismantle a few of them.

Myth #1: The Shark Lawyers

Lawyers are only interested in winning. They live in their heads and don't care about the pain they cause people. They cruise around like sharks, waiting for the smell of blood. Then they attack, straight for the throat. The weaker the victim, the better. Winning is everything.

We live in a warrior culture, where men in particular are socialized from infancy to see life as a contest. The raw material of the world's events is seen through the patriarchal filters of dualism (us or them, this choice or that, this idea or that) and hierarchy (we are better than them, this choice is more worthy than that).

People who become lawyers are formally trained to see issues as us/them, one-up/one-down. The legal system itself is modeled on the contest, with the lawyer mandated to perform as the professional combatant, there to win.

In the child welfare field the shark-lawyer stereotype gains extra energy from the alienation social workers experience when they confront the legal system. The notion of life as nothing but a contest is offensive to many in the helping professions, whose training embodies different belief systems entirely.

For social workers, protecting kids has to do with trying to help people discover solutions to their problems in whatever way will enable each family member to "win." The toolbag includes communication, creating bridges, fostering alliances and building alternatives. The world is envisioned as a web of human interconnectedness, rather than as a ladder of hierarchies.

The alienation experienced by social workers when these two belief systems collide is exacerbated by the "tough" orientation of the combatant lawyer. The reality he is concerned with—the only one he will see as relevant to the contest—is the world of "facts." Information deriving from nonobjective sources—inner reality, intuition, spirituality—is seen not only as irrelevant, but inherently "false."

Faced with a lawyer who sees a protection case in win-lose terms, and who invalidates much of the information she sees as important, a social worker can be tempted to swallow the shark-lawyer stereotype without even chewing. Seeing lawyers this way achieves separation, not only from the hostility of individual lawyers but from a battleplace mentality that does not seem to include much love. This choice is toxic, however, in the sense that it renders the social worker powerless to truly engage the lawyer.

Dismantling the myth involves three steps:

1. *Acknowledging* how much you have chosen to see the lawyer in terms of the stereotype;
2. Creating ways to *protect yourself* from an alien belief system;
3. Discovering the *common ground* between yourself and the lawyer: the places where the two belief systems overlap.

The first step involves seeing the lawyer's adversarial behavior as an entity distinct from the lawyer as a person. Acknowledging one's distaste for the aggressive stance is a way of making visible the force which drives the stereotype. It brings the stereotype itself into the light, to be seen for what it is. The lawyer *does* operate under the value system of the contest model, obliged at times to seem the shark. But the only teeth he has are those you give him.

Self-protection comes from controlling your own personal boundaries when hostility and aggression are offered up for consumption. Seeing the lawyer as acting *for* his belief system and not *against* you keeps you separate from his behavior.

As a social worker you are already experienced in not absorbing the behaviors of hostile and resistant parents. You allow yourself to remain aware of these energies but keep them outside your personal boundaries so that the parent remains visible as a person. You know that if you take them personally, you automatically place yourself in a limiting reactive position instead of a constructive, responsive one.

The same technique works *just as well* when you are under harsh cross-examination by an apparently hostile lawyer. As with resistant parents, the hostility is merely offered up, along with the toxic power embedded in it. *You always have the choice to respond to the question without reacting to the tone in which it is asked.*

The living experience of the child before the court is the common ground between yourself and the lawyer you are dealing with. This is where the two belief systems overlap. The task is to create communication bridges between yourself and the lawyer which neither threaten his belief system nor invalidate your own. As with any communication, you must speak the language of the other in order to be understood. To make the child's life situation real to the lawyer, you must speak in terms acceptable to his belief system: concrete facts, objective observations, sensory images of the child's experiences. Offering up interpretations and opinions about the facts, particularly in the professional jargon of your field, will not only ring alarm bells in the belief system of the lawyer about what is "relevant," but will also summon up the shark within.

Seeing a lawyer in terms of the mythology makes him a personal adversary rather than simply a part of an adversarial system. Seeing the human being behind the stereotype transforms the adversary into a potential ally. As allies, you have the power to enable the lawyer to understand the helper belief system and he may offer the bonus of insights about the mechanics of his own belief system. This can only happen on the dry land of awareness, not in the dark place where sharks are circling. That is only a mythological place, after all.

Myth #2: The Big Daddy Judge

Judges are supposed to be neutral and fair, aren't they? We should be able to rely on their wisdom. When the judge criticizes me, it seems unfair. I don't think some of the judges even like children. I *know* some of them don't like social workers.

As the ultimate decision-maker in the legal system, the judge, male or female, is the father-figure incarnate. He is an important symbol in a patriarchal culture, about whom we have high expectations. The distance between the mythical image and the day-to-day courtroom reality is sometimes painfully felt by social workers.

The falsity of the Big Daddy Judge myth lies in the unrealistic expectations upon which it is based. All of us have a deep need for there to be *someone* who can give us the answers, solve our problems, and make everything okay. The legal system fosters the myth that the all-knowing judge can play this superhuman role. Daddy knows best.

This image of the judge obscures the reality of his job in protection cases. The judge *knows* the legal system has never been very good at solving problems of human relations. The forte of the law, after all, is resolving disputes about objective events which have occurred in the past, particularly transactions involving money. Deciding protection cases involves predicting future human relations, a task for which neither the judge nor the legal system may be suited. But the judge, being a judge, is not realistically in a position to complain about the limitations of the system he represents.

As a former lawyer, the judge has also been trained to honor the contest model with its either-or slant on reality. He may be very well aware that his analytical training is often not much help in responding to families in crisis, who behave neither rationally nor logically. Again, the judge is not realistically in a position to acknowledge the inherent limitations of his own training.

The legal system is the check-and-balance to your discretion as a social worker. But the judge is subject to his own check-and-balance, which is the set of restrictions on the kind of information available to him. The technical rules of evidence and procedure control his access to information on which the decision is made. You may have very relevant information which the judge *does not have the option to hear,* because it offends the rules. Contrary to the myth of the Big Daddy Judge, he can't just do what he thinks "right." And when he prevents you from saying something, he isn't necessarily doing it just to be disagreeable.

Still, a judge may *be* outright disagreeable at times. The psychological reality of his job is that in important ways, he cannot say what he feels, he cannot react personally, he cannot readily ventilate his anger or frustration, and he cannot be seen to complain about the unworkable limitations that often circumscribe the choices available to him.

The job creates a good deal of undischarged negative energy. Occasionally this energy leaks out onto the social worker on the witness stand. Sometimes the worker is simply handy; sometimes she inadvertently provokes the discharge.

For example, a social worker who is "certain" that she "feels" that a child is abused gives the judge information which is unacceptable to the system he represents. A worker who says that something "appears" or "seems" to have occurred makes the judge wonder at her apparent uncertainty. A worker who "shares" rather than "tells," or who prefers professional jargon to clear, specific, well-organized evidence merely contributes to the stereotype of social workers as inadequate witnesses. Notice your own terminology. Is it inadvertently inflammatory?

Judges are human but the judging *role* is super-human. Judges get cranky. They get up on the wrong side of the bed. They experience dislike of particular individuals. They get frustrated with social workers who have not developed a working familiarity with the limitations of the legal system and of the choices available to judges.

The judge has the power and the responsibility to make the decision, but of necessity has less to go on than is sometimes needed. Releasing yourself from the myth of the calm, all-knowing judge enables both you and the judge to focus on the task at hand. Like you, the judge is doing the best he can with the resources he has. He also has a personal need to be respected in this light. Whether the judge in the particular case is your ally or your enemy depends more upon how you see his role than on who he is as an individual.

Myth #3: The Intimidating Courtroom

I get rattled when I walk into the courtroom. The physical space makes me uncomfortable. I don't like the feeling of the judge sitting higher than everyone else. No matter how much preparation I do I'm still a wreck by the time I get onto the witness stand.

The courtroom is *designed* to be intimidating. Where would we be if people thought courtrooms were just one more place to fuss about things? What would a king be without his castle? Just another guy.

We are talking here about symbols and settings. Polished wood, oak paneling, crests and insignia. Robes and suits. Flags and thick books with small print. The desire of courtroom designers is to render the dignity and majesty of the law. You are intended to *feel* the presence of authority when you walk into a courtroom.

The hidden agenda is to create enough fear to motivate people to exercise self-control. Courts exercise real power; they have the right to *demand*, over and above your own power to persuade, to suggest. The quickest way to communicate power is physically, through the formality of the setting itself.

Even the tackiest, most threadbare family courts successfully intimidate visitors to them. The most diminutive judges swell with authority by sitting higher than anyone else in the room. The courtroom itself says, "What happens here counts. Be careful what you do."

The stereotype of the frightening courtroom is one of the easiest to dismantle. The goal is to put the intimidation factor into perspective, so that the physical space becomes a comfortable part of your working territory. Reclaim the portions of your power that the intimidation factor has removed by trying the following:

1. Recognize that everyone experiences the intimidation factor to some degree. The courtroom is a stage, and even the best actors get

stagefright. Good actors, like good lawyers and good witnesses, just don't let you see it.

2. Familiarity breeds familiarity. Get comfortable with the place, which, after all, is just a room. Take the time to observe other cases. Visit the court when it is empty. Ask the court staff to show you around behind the scenes.

3. Check out superior courts to get a sense of grander versions of the standard layout. Put your own courtroom into perspective.

4. Walk in the judge's mocassins. Borrow a robe and try it on for size. Get permission to sit on the judge's bench for awhile when court is not in session. What does the place look like from his perspective?

In short, do anything you need to in order to get comfortable with the place. Notice if your throat tightens when you enter the courtroom. Be aware of your physical reactions to the space and give yourself permission to experience them. Consciousness of *reactions* opens the door to alternative *responses*.

The goal is *not* to neutralize the sense of intimidation to the point that the courtroom feels the same as the staff coffee room.

The goal is to *own* the feeling of the court to the point that it becomes another part of the whole territory where you do your work. Other places you have to go have intimidating aspects to them. Like court, they are *part of your territory.*

Myth #4: The Lottery Justice System

The law has so many rules it's hard to tell the whole story. You never know what the judge is going to decide. Maybe the court does the best it can, but it's still a crap shoot. Too often the kid is the real loser.

Everyone knocks the justice system from time to time. Its occasional foul-ups provoke instant notoriety and justifiable outrage. Its defects *are* real.

The unpredictability of it all causes sleepless nights for many a social worker. Why is the justice system often unpredictable, and what can be done about the sleepless nights?

1. Expectations are Unrealistic

The only perfect solution to disputes is to avoid them in the first place. When disputes are taken to court, we are socialized to believe that the justice system should be able to determine *all* of the truth *all* of the time, and *always* make the "right" decision.

We get offended when the human face of the justice system presents itself, with all its fallibility. But, for all its pretensions, the justice system is merely another human system. It produces absolutely perfect justice as often as you produce absolutely perfect social work. It is understandable to expect perfection of it, but it is also unreasonable. Expecting perfection often implies a need to experience disappointment, which merely confirms fears.

2. Honor the Limitations

The justice system has defects enough without being trashed for not magically divining the essence of a case. The justice system can *only* make decisions based on legal evidence provable in a court of law. Feelings, intuitions, suspicions, and gossip (hearsay: secondhand information) do not advance *legal* cases.

The task is to *verify* concerns with *provable* facts. This is an onerous job; sometimes it is easier to fault the system for not acting on our dead-on hunches than to *prove* those hunches are correct. When this happens the child *is* the loser, all right, but the justice system is the scapegoat, not the perpetrator.

3. Honor the Power

Some social workers get possessive about their cases.

The attitude that develops, which is quickly picked up by the other players in the justice system (whether they say so or not), is that only the social worker knows best.

Noticing the toxic effect of this attitude is not incompatible with observing at the same time that often the social worker *does* know best. She has, after all, a whole wealth of information to go on, much of which is unacceptable to a court of law.

The problem with taking this attitude to court is that if a social worker wants to be regarded as a professional witness, she must be seen to honor the reality that society has *divided* the power to protect kids. The social worker has the power to remove the child, but this action triggers the power of the justice system to make the final decisions.

The working reality is that once your case goes to court and you walk through the courtroom door, your job has changed. At that point you are no longer ultimately responsible for the child; the justice system is. You are there to present your observations and concerns, but the final decision is no longer yours.

This shift in power is real, and needs to be both acknowledged and honored. To *challenge* the shift in power, to suggest that the justice system should not have the power ultimately to determine the fate of children, is an act of politics, not social work. Second-guessing the court is a fast track to burnout. There are already enough unavoidable aspects of the social work job which contribute to burnout without adding to them a habitual cynicism about the justice system.

4. Keeping your Distance

Not every case can be "won." Not every child can be protected, in court or out. Not every result will be fair.

To see things otherwise is to mistake the *ideals* of perfect justice and perfect safety for every child for the *reality* that all that can really be done is for each player in the process to do his or her best. The very real shortcomings and failures can invalidate the equally real good that is actually accomplished, if you let them.

The temptation to lose faith is strong at times. Carnage does occur and the justice system doesn't always serve its own ideals. But rejection of the system outright is often a result of not keeping a healthy distance from the job. You *need* to maintain a sufficient distance to keep visible the eternal difference between what is preferable and what is possible.

Myth #5: The Hopeless Parent

People have kids without the first clue about how to take care of them. The parents I see are so wrapped up with their own personal problems, it's a wonder the kids survive at all.

The territory of families in crisis breeds understandable cynicism. The myth of the hopeless parent serves to soften the pain by anticipating it.

When you observe the myth in operation in others, you have a choice of responses. Initial reactions of anger and judgment need to be gently set aside in order to work through the power of the myth.

Notice *who* has bought the myth. Court staff and some lawyers who are temperamentally unsuited to the field sometimes swallow the myth whole, as a coping mechanism. The toxic effect of this myth is its special dynamic of blame. Blaming alone doesn't help. It only isolates those who need help.

In your testimony you can neutralize the myth and restore balance to the way in which the parents are seen. You can speak the good that you see in the parents, so that others can see it. And you can present their problems in a way that keeps hope alive, by being clear and specific about the *achievable* responsibilities that need to be met. This may be a narrow path to tread. Choose your words with care.

Occasionally you may notice the myth gaining energy somewhere *inside* yourself. When you find yourself starting to *see* parents as hopeless, almost from the outset, it may be a signal that it is time to check out whether you have drifted past your own thresholds of tolerance. You may need to take a holiday, or to pamper yourself in some way, or just to talk things out with someone sympathetic.

As a social worker you operate in a very slim human margin sometimes. You need to give yourself permission to celebrate small gains, even though they may seem trivial to those working the other side of the street.

The myth of the hopeless parent removes power and choices from the parent, in the same way that your own power and choices are diminished when you are seen as merely part of a faceless bureaucracy. (In fact these two myths sometimes walk hand in hand. Check out how *you* are seen by those who see the parents as hopeless.)

The danger is that these myths appeal to the natural human tendency to live up to (or down to) expectations. Speaking the good you see in the parents adds to their choices, which releases power and adds to choices available to the child. Making the parents real to the court helps to make them real to the child.

Myth #6: The Steamrollered Child

The legal system says it is there to protect the child, but so often the child seems to become invisible in the dust created by the adversarial system. When grownups fight, the needs of the kid don't get met. That's a fact, in court or out.

Why does the child disappear in the heat of battle?

One reason the child sometimes seems to be steamrollered through the legal system is that other agendas are in play at the same time.

Notice the words used within the legal process. The judge must "dispose" of his cases. The parents' lawyer is mandated to "fight" for her clients. Your lawyer is under pressure to complete his "list." Items relevant to the child's life are "exhibits" to be "filed." For the "case" to be "dealt with," each of the "parties" is oriented to completion of his own agenda.

None of these words evokes the pain of the child. All of them support a myth of the child being processed by an unresponsive administrative system.

Well, it can't happen unless you let it. Every time you are asked a question in court, whether by the judge, your own lawyer, or under cross-examination, you have the opportunity to make the child's life real.

This is why your own words are so important. "The baby had a diaper rash" conveys the objective reality with the same absence of emotional content as words describing aspects of the legal process. "The baby had a vivid red rash, crusted at the edges, extending from his navel to his hips and entirely covering his genitals and buttocks" makes the child's *experience* real in the minds of all players in the legal process.

The *sensory images* you evoke with your choice of words are the antidote to the child being steamrollered. The myth is that when the legal process is in full flight, the child won't be clearly seen. The truth is that this can only happen if you allow *yourself* to be swept away: your only task in court, when it gets right down to it, is to make the child's life real in the mind of the judge. All else is windowdressing; *you* are the window.

Myth #7: The Oversensitive Social Worker

I get real angry when lawyers imply that I'm too emotional to see things objectively. Or when a judge looks at me as if to say, "Well, here comes another wimpy social worker." Sometimes I feel like nobody is really listening to me or believing what I have to say. I end up feeling totally invalidated.

It's best to deal with this one head-on.

Of course you're over-sensitive. What kind of people-helper would you be if you didn't have the extra sensitivity, the hyper-intuition, that allows you to pick up extra signals in the complex process of human relations in crisis? It is your sensitivity that *enables* you TO CONNECT with people, and understand.

The stereotype derives from this aspect of the reputation of social workers, but the intention of it is to put-down, maliciously. The meaning conveyed is that as a social worker you are prone to vague and fluffy wallowing in emotion, to flying off the handle over trivia, to naively ignoring the hard edges of "reality."

There are four segments of the stereotype that deserve a closer look:

1. The Source of the Bile

We live in a society which is easily threatened by the emotional world. From childhood we are encouraged to achieve "self-control" and to "get a grip on our feelings." Many otherwise "normal" adults are walking emotional amputees, out of touch with what their hearts say.

Fear about feelings is normative in our culture. Considering that social workers deal with very scary feelings on a daily basis, it is no surprise that they are often treated dismissively or regarded with deep suspicion by those who have the most difficulty connecting with their own emotional world.

These reactions, based on fear, need not be taken personally unless you choose to do so.

2. The Credibility Factor

To maintain credibility within the linear world of the dualistic legal system, you must choose to meet it half-way. Premonitions, suspicions and intuitions are not forms of information which the legal system is designed to ingest. Even in referring to "objective" facts, a social worker who chooses "mushy" language or jargon undermines her own credibility.

The legal system requires clear, specific, organized presentations of provable facts. The trick is to *start* with your oversensitive intuitions about what is going on, but to *consciously select* the information you will use in your testimony. The goal is not to ignore the intuitions, but to identify the *facts* which validate them. In effect, you are translating your intuitions into language which the system can readily ingest.

The effort required is not enormous, but some concrete effort must be made—credibility is earned, not granted.

3. The Briefing Factor

Along with their fetish for factual details, players in the legal system also love brevity and metaphor. In briefing your counsel, a sixty-second precis of the dynamic you see operating within the family can put your lawyer into the essence of the picture more readily than twenty pages of casenotes. If the "real" issue as you see it is that the mother just can't stand kids once they get past the toddler stage, tell your lawyer. Give him a sense of the forest as well as the trees.

The distinction here is between testifying in court and preparing for the case before court. The stereotype can serve you in dealing with counsel out of court because lawyers on both sides struggle to get a grasp on what is really going on. As a social worker, your insights are valuable shortcuts to understanding; whether they are acceptable as testimony is a separate question.

4. Intuition in Court

Observing family members in the new context of the courtroom dynamic generates additional insights into their behaviors. The tendency is to keep these to yourself, because they are not "evidence."

Deciding how to present the case in court (what evidence to call, which witness to call next, how to handle the summation) is a management task for your counsel, one in which he calls regularly upon his own intuition (although he may prefer to call it "professional judgment"). You are likely to pick up subtle signals he is missing. He will present a stronger case if you choose to share your insights as you go along.

There is a grain of truth in every stereotype. When you find yourself cast in the stereotype of the oversensitive social worker, you are also being presented with a choice between reacting defensively or responding in a way that enables the energy of the stereotype to work for you, and for the case.

BEYOND THE SCAPEGOAT SYNDROME

Some social workers never move beyond the state of shock created by their first court case. A victim mentality sets in, with each further case amounting to "proof" that they cannot be effective in court. The judge is too mean, the lawyers too vicious, the justice system too crazy, and the parents are hopeless anyway.

Workers who spend a lot of time in the victim stance at court like to tell war stories afterwards. These serve to dissipate the tension that the victim stance creates, without having to acknowledge any responsibility for the results in court. The lawyers were vicious and so forth because that's just the way they are, not because the worker's testimony was vague and unprepared, or because she chose to take every negative comment personally, or because she spent so much time reacting that the child remained invisible. "I did my best, but what can you do?"

The scapegoat syndrome operates in court just as it does in families. In abusive families a child is often chosen as the scapegoat, the carrier of the burden of grief and conflict in each of the other family members. Blaming the scapegoat child for everything that is wrong in the family is an effective way for every other family member to disown personal responsibility for his own problems.

By choosing to see the judge, the lawyers, the courtroom, the justice system, the parents or the child in mythological or stereotypical terms, these parts become scapegoats of the protection process as a whole. As within abusive families, the unconscious goal is to disown responsibility for one's own contribution to difficulty by seeing shortfalls everywhere but in oneself.

All of the myths and stereotypes about the legal system are true, in the sense that there are real defects involved. All of them are also false, in the way they treat the elements of the system simplistically. The myths and stereotypes extract a high price, as each of them removes choices about how to respond.

To be effective in court, you need to be able to respond, fully. This includes remaining conscious of those things you might have done differently, or better. Notice whether you make use of the myths and stereotypes as a way of disengaging from your own mistakes. Indeed, consider whether you have given yourself permission to make mistakes and to learn from them.

Scapegoating other elements in the collective endeavour is toxic, as it amounts to giving power away instead of exercising it. Power involves choices made in the field of reality; myths and stereotypes remove choices by replacing the field of reality with fantasies.

As you move through the myths and stereotypes to the actual people and real, limited systems behind them, you also make this territory part of your own. As a resident of the territory, you regain your freedom to respond to actual people and real events. Noticing the energy you have invested in the traditional myths and stereotypes of the legal system is the first step in reclaiming it for more useful purposes.

The fact is that there are a great many effective, concrete techniques available to social workers who deal with lawyers and court, and many alternatives to call upon if a particular approach isn't working. The following chapters detail a variety of practical options which are readily at hand. But to put them in your toolbag, you first need to let go of the myths and reclaim the power you have given over to them.

Take back your power. You'll need it!

Chapter 2

PROTECTING KIDS:
HELP WANTED, HELP UNWANTED

CLICHES ABOUT CARING FOR KIDS

Dick and Jane did a job on all of us.

Do you remember Dick and Jane? They lived in the school readers of a generation ago. Dad smoked a pipe and went to work. Mom stayed home and happily cooked and cleaned in her spotless kitchen. Dick and Jane walked to school on immaculate sidewalks, innocent and content. Little sister Sally stayed adorably at home, playing with the family dog, Spot, and the orange kitten, Puff. Go, Puff, Go!

One of Dick and Jane's peak experiences occurred in the autumn when friendly old Zeke, the neighborhood maintenance man, raked up all the leaves on Pleasant Street and made a huge bonfire. The whole neighbourhood gathered to watch in the crisp autumn evening. At the end of it all, good old Zeke raked the embers aside and—surprise! Baked potatoes for everyone, wrapped in aluminum foil.

If Pleasant Street existed in modern children's stories, Dick would fail to turn in his class project on time because he would be too obsessive about playing video games on the television in his bedroom; his step-sister, Jane, would be cranky after access visits with her real Dad, because she didn't get along with Dad's new girlfriend; and Zeke would constantly run the risk of arrest due to his questionable interest in kids!

The accelerated rate of social change over the last two generations has revolutionized the institution of the family. One symbol of change is the statistic that in 1987 one child in 34 was reported abused or neglected. Pleasant Street is no more, if it ever was.

We are a society which has yet to come fully to terms with what we are doing to our children. As the number of reports of abuse and neglect escalates, there is a tendency to seek comfort in the fantasies of family life generated in the euphoric fifties.

In child protection work these fantasies come in the form of child-

21

rearing cliches, tossed at your feet. Unlike the myths and stereotypes of the legal system discussed in the previous chapter, the parenting cliches do not have to be probed too deeply. But you do need to notice their appearance and make a conscious decision about how to deal with them as you go along.

Here are four examples of the kind of bromides you will run into time and again. You can surely add to the list from your own experience.

- All kids need is love.
- Real parents know better than childless people.
- Parenting is mainly a matter of instinct.
- We all love and honor children.

You get the idea. Platitudes will tend to be cited inside and outside the legal system in defense of your allegation that parental conduct has put a child at risk. The purpose behind throwing these articles of faith at you is to divert attention from the issues at hand by moving the focus from examining specific events to debating parenting in general.

We know a lot more about the dynamics of parenting and families than we did a generation or two ago. If you want to, you can choose to cite this knowledge if you wish, to put living flesh on the bare bones of the cliches. You can explain that kids do need love, of course, but they also need stability, consistency, regular meals, *time:* good intentions don't really count. You can point out that although parenting has its mystical dimensions, much of it consists of concrete, learnable skills, although no training or education in them is required before people have kids. You can observe that vast numbers of kids are unwanted, illiterate, on the streets, or have kids of their own before they are out of childhood themselves. You can mention which age group has the highest suicide rate.

And so forth.

The question is not whether there are ways to articulate visions of parenting which demonstrate the flaws in the standard cliches. The question is whether it is worthwhile for you to enter the debate at all.

Your removal of a child from his family incidentally provokes defense of closely held beliefs about what raising a family means. These beliefs are deeply cherished, despite the fact that many of them are empty of real meaning today. In a sense, the need for social workers to remove children is an affront to our favorite collective notions and fantasies about happy family life. You are the harbinger of deeply unsettling news about the institution of the family.

Watch for the subtle air of desperation sometimes accompanying the defense of child-rearing cliches. In addition to disrupting the particular family, your intervention also disrupts the family's old belief systems and challenges their adequacy. It is as if the problem would be easier to cope with if only you would offer reassurance that the old truths can still be relied upon. How dare you not only remove the child, but also claim that instinct is not enough?

How dare you indeed!

We think we know a lot about what doesn't work in families, and what would help. But we also know that some kids can transcend appalling home lives and flourish, and others self-destruct in the face of ample love and support. The psychological study of families generates conflicting theories and few certainties. We know that the simple truths of former generations have somehow not protected large numbers of our children from abuse and neglect. We also know that people tend to seek comfort in the simple truths rather than confront the awful reality of what is happening to many of our children. None of this territory is comfortable for anyone.

When motherhood statements are presented in defense, you are not obliged to trot out your own personal and professional stock of pet theories about why the modern family is in a state of crisis. The nature of your job is such that you will be invited to articulate aspects of the larger picture from time to time. Exercise discretion about accepting these invitations. This is deep water to navigate successfully. And notice that every debate about parenting theory moves the focus away from the concrete reality of *this* case, *this* family, *this* child.

Often it is just as well to allow motherhood statements to pass without comment. If you do elect to enter the fray, be direct, concise, and unapologetic for your own views, to which you are entitled. And notice how long it takes you to move on to your primary purpose: to speak out about what *this* kid needs *now.*

KIDS AS PROPERTY

A regular television joke about family life is that kids are "mine" when they're good and "yours" when they're bad, as in, "Why don't you tell *your* son to finish his supper?" There is a legal version of the concept of kids as possessions, which is revealed most vividly in divorce battles. Good-faith custody disputes seriously question who is the better parent for the kids. Bad-faith ones use the dispute purportedly about custody as a vehicle for one adult to express outrage to the other adult, with the intent of making the other adult's life as miserable as possible. Malicious allegations of sexual abuse are the ultimate weapon in bad faith custody disputes. These allegations usually escalate the destruction of family relationships beyond repair.

The law attempts to create rational mechanisms to guide resolution of disputes, referred to as "tests." In a private custody dispute, the test is what is in the best interests of the child. Many courts have tried to define the elements of the test in ways that make the decision-making process seem more analytical and rational, but it all comes down to the subjective decision of the particular judge in the end.

In protection cases there are two tests. First, is there sufficient evidence to show that the child was at such risk that his removal from his family was justified? Second, if removal is found to be justified, is it in the best interests of the child that he be returned home on some basis, or that he remain in the care of the agency?

Later chapters will detail how to present evidence that addresses the tests used by the court in protection cases. The purpose of this section is to note, by way of perspective, how closely the legal system parallels the child-as-property orientation of many parents locked in private custody battles.

When you strip away the conceptual dressing, the court in a protection case is ultimately deciding whether the parent or the agency should "own" the child. To push the property metaphor ever so slightly, a return home under supervision is a little like rent-to-purchase: if the contract goes okay, you get to keep the object. A six-month wardship order is analogous to a temporary lease. At the end of the lease period, the object is returned to its original owner. A permanent order leading to adoption has the flavor of finality that is characteristic of any final transfer of ownership of property.

The property orientation of the law is not surprising when you consider that the original function of the law historically was to govern ownership of things. The courts have had centuries of experience in deciding who owns what and for how long. And for much of that history, the legal system never questioned the legal right of the natural father to absolute ownership of his children. In the historical scale of things, custody and protection of children are relatively recent threads in an ancient legal fabric devoted to deciding ownership of things.

The best private custody arrangements, created by the parents themselves without the assistance of the legal system, offer perspective at the other end of the spectrum. Mom and Dad, though separated, honor the commitment embodied by the creation of their child. They communicate regularly, maintain a flexible stance, and go out of their way to accommodate each other where the child is concerned. Mom has an invitation that she would like to accept and Dad takes the child an extra evening, with the tacit understanding that he can expect similar flexibility. Each honors the rules of the house in the other home without feeling that different values and standards must be homogenized. The child is made a part of the give-and-take necessary for the adults to form new relationships, without sacrificing loyalties or adult needs.

These arrangements don't hit the front pages, but they exist in abundance. The vital component is a mutual acknowledgement of a form of permanent love between the adults in their ongoing roles as parents of the same child. It isn't always easy, but it's very possible, given a healthy dose of goodwill and maturity, and a willingness to make the child a priority.

And the heartening aspect, the one that confounds much of the standard literature, is how the child thrives. Kids adapt positively to the two different value systems, the two sets of house rules, the two sets of expectations. The "conflict" between the two houses doesn't seem to be *felt* by kids unless the *adults* choose to make an issue of them. Moving frequently between the two environments can be no more traumatic than going from home to school, a far more drastic change of environment. Nothing at home prepares the child for the strange notion that you have have to raise your hand before you can ask a question. The child has little difficulty picking up such a radical shift in the rules. The difference between home and school is not experienced as particularly stressful. If, however, the teacher started telling the child his parent *should* make him raise his hand at home as well, that's when the child would experience the difference as pain.

The child-oriented private custody arrangement described above is analogous to the voluntary steps you encourage in the family before intervention or court action is contemplated. As with the best custody arrangements, fostering voluntary change involves a similar angst of help wanted, help unwanted. The ambivalence in your cases is intensified by the parents' awareness that you have the power to invoke the sanction of the law if required.

Successful family functioning requires frequent tinkering and adjustments, whether the family is "intact" or not. Within the limitations of your resources, the variations of your assistance to a family are limitless and can be *custom-designed to meet the needs of the child.*

Once the protection issue needs to be dealt with in court, the ball game changes. Orders can be varied and fine-tuned, but basically the court has fixed, limited options that are considered, decided upon, and imposed to accomodate an adult time scale. What you gain in "persuasive" power by invoking the authority of the law you lose in the law's bent for dealing with the complex needs of kids as if ownership were the primary question. It is not, of course, and the courts and lawyers know that, but the law is a blunt tool at the best of times. You will still need the more refined tools in your professional toolbag to help the child in ways not available in court.

LET THE SOCIAL WORKERS TAKE CARE OF IT, AS LONG AS THEY DON'T DO ANYTHING

With one hand, society mandates you to help families. The other hand is used to place obstacles in your way. Caseloads in many agency offices are too large to permit the time each family needs. Support services for the family are limited. Some agencies are more devoted to collecting reports of abuse and neglect than they are to servicing the families who are reported. The resources available only go so far.

The ambivalence about enabling you to do your job effectively has partly to do with how your job evolved. In many other societies, notably ones we characterize as "primitive" according to our technological yardstick, the community as a whole is directly responsible for the welfare of its young. Our own society of a generation or two ago shared this sense of responsibility with and for our neighbors. Today, when a neighbor is in trouble, we call the appropriate authorities. You are one of the authorities.

One of the consequences of letting someone else be responsible to deal with social problems is that as a society, we no longer have to deal with the problems as citizens in a community. The government has said it will help abused and neglected kids, so let the social workers get on with it. The problem is, by definition, taken care of. It is flushed away.

The ambivalence is intensified by the fact that as a society, we have not yet come to terms with the dilemma of parental rights versus children's rights. We have no social consensus about children's rights at all, rhetoric aside. Parental rights tend to be seen in terms of our powerful traditions of individual freedom and privacy, so it is not surprising that there is anxiety about the notion that the state, which is what you represent, is entitled to worm its way into the homes and bedrooms of the nation. Freedom and privacy seem at stake, and they are.

Social concern about parental rights results in a growing technicality of procedure evolving about how and when you are entitled to exercise your power to remove a child. And when you get to court, you are fettered by technical rules, applied with splendid inconsistency, about what information is acceptable to present. Finally, if you succeed in proving that the child requires care, the resources are so limited as to raise the question of whether the child is any better off.

As a society we all agree that the problem of neglected and abused children is a terrible disgrace, and we could, if we wished, assign resources to do something about root causes. Instead, you are left to deal with things on a case-by-case basis. It is this "firefighter" element of your job that causes many of your colleagues eventually to leave the field in discouragement. After awhile it just gets tiring. The negativity and suspicion with which you are greeted eats away at the soul. The craziness of being mandated to protect kids by a society that sets roadblocks at every turn gets to be too much.

The ambivalence about whether we really want you to be able to do the task you have been assigned shows up in the courtroom as much as anywhere else. It is part of the court function to make you accountable for the discretion you exercise, but sometimes the experience on the witness stand suggests that the real purpose is to make you justify every action, verify every allegation, explore every option, anticipate every problem. Sometimes you feel on trial yourself, well beyond the point of being required to be accountable. Sometimes the response of the legal system to your job is enough to make you wonder whether you and the legal system are, in fact, involved in the collective goal of trying to protect kids.

Deep-seated ambivalence about what you do goes with the territory. Officially, you have the full backing of the government and the people, of the legal system and its players. But unofficially, your work is one more nagging reminder that society seems to be going to hell in a handbasket. You seem to bring only bad news, without end.

All you can do is take the obstacles in stride. It will take a long time for society to come to terms with why it is trashing so many of its children.

Until it does, the resources needed to *prevent* child abuse and neglect will not be provided. Meanwhile it is your task to deal with the tip of the iceberg when it shows through, and simply accept that society is deeply ambivalent about your work.

In court, be prepared to explain the alternatives considered. Demonstrate care about actions taken, avoid allegations without provable evidence. Present your game plan; be specific about the problems and the options. Be frank about the limitations of what you can do. You will still receive gratuitous disapproval occasionally, no matter what. Recognize that this occurs, at least in part, because your work exposes the failure of society to honor its children. This failure is not easy for anyone to face. You don't have to pretend that society's ambivalence about what it is doing to its children doesn't impair what you can accomplish, but you don't have to take the burden of ambivalence on your own shoulders, either.

COVERT COERCION

The court exercises bald power, openly. Your own power is more covert. On the face of things, you foster a helping relationship with the family; you encourage, influence, and persuade. Both you and the parents tacitly agree to pretend that your presence in the home is invited and the responses to your suggestions are voluntary.

The covert part is, of course, that if need be you have the power to take away the child.

With rare exceptions, no one else in our society has the power to enter into a private home at any hour and take away someone's child. The very idea of a society in which government employees have such powers smacks of totalitarian regimes, until we recall that the driving force behind your power is not weapons, wealth, or political paranoia; just kids.

Still, your power is daunting.

Your ultimate power to remove the child can have a therapeutic effect all by itself. Awareness of this power can enable a parent to transcend the denial and resistance, and focus on the realities at hand. The courts sometimes use the presence of their authority in the same therapeutic way. Some judges are adept at giving parents advice or direction from the bench, using the authority of their office to nudge the parents in the right direction.

The double-bind for the social worker is you are both ally and potential adversary at the same time. As an ally, you build trust in the working relationship with the family, and seek confidences. As adversary, you have the power to remove the child and to reveal confidences in a court of law. Where these two sides of your role have not been discussed with the parent, the cost is a loss of trust in the future working relationship.

Frankness is the better course. Bring both sides of your role out into the open.

A gradually deteriorating situation is no place to pretend that your requests for action are as voluntary as they might once have been. When you are approaching the point where removal of the child will likely be necessary, tell the parent what is in store. Because of the power differential between yourself and the parent, it is not reasonable to expect the parent to raise the issue of whether you are considering removal. In fairness, you need to raise the issue yourself. Removal of a child is a serious step. Ordinarily this step should not be taken without prior warning to the parent, or without a clear, specific communication of the achievable steps that must be taken if removal is to be avoided.

If your agency has no policy on this point, you need to develop one for yourself. On balance, be overt about how the power to remove a child is exercised, and under what circumstances, once that course of action becomes a realistic possibility. Be careful, and clear. Making your power overt must be done in a way that embodies the fairness of being open and giving notice, without any tenor of making a threat. (It may be *perceived* as a threat sometimes anyway, but you can't help that. In court, you can testify about how you handled the situation and the judge will make his own decision about whether you were being fair or bullying.)

This is delicate stuff. It is analogous to the unfairness problem of hidden expectations. If we are not told what we are expected to do, we feel a keen sense of injustice if we are later faulted for not meeting the hidden expectations.

It is understandable that neither you nor the parent want to talk about removal of the child unless absolutely necessary. You still need to create a policy to guide you, to ensure that you *do* discuss removal when it is fair and appropriate that you do so. Otherwise, your actions may be later portrayed in court tainted with an aroma of ambush. Be fair. Be seen to be fair.

MEDIA THIRST FOR FASHIONABLE CASES

The media play a powerful role in raising consciousness about the plight of kids. Poverty and neglect are not dramatic enough to get anything like the attention they deserve in terms of the extent of the problem. The truly horrific neglect cases garner wide publicity, but neglect cases per se receive little media attention. Sexual and physical abuse of children is thought far more newsworthy. Sexual abuse cases in particular command instant public attention. Sensational cases get full nationwide treatment on a regular basis. In terms of promoting social consciousness about children at risk, this is unfortunate, in the sense that far more children need protection from neglect than from abuse. The public cannot be expected to understand how grave the problem of neglect really is, since the media largely ignore the subject.

When media representatives decide that one of your cases is newsworthy, a new dimension is added to your role. You will be asked to make public statements. You are subject to agency policy about the contact you can have with the media when a case receives media attention. In most situations you are likely to be expected to keep your lip buttoned tight, and to leave the articulation of the agency position to senior colleagues mandated for the task, or to your counsel as the agency's representative.

If you do have a case that commands media attention, make use of your network of colleagues for support. Testifying in court is often strain enough, without knowing that your words will appear in the next day's newspaper for interpretation by all.

Speaking to the media directly is an art form unto itself. The successful are those who understand its parameters, and who know that conflict is the driving force behind every good news story. The logistical limitation of a few seconds of television time or a paragraph or two in a news story means that the "facts" need to be boiled down to their starkest elements. The media also prefer to hear those facts which heighten the sense of conflict between opposing sides. Deft media handlers feed this penchant and come off strong. The naive just "tell the truth" and are shocked by the slant presented when only portions of the whole statement are actually quoted.

Media excitement about occasional cases goes with your territory, but dealing with the media directly probably does not. If you are not absolutely sure that you know what you are doing and that you have authorization, you probably don't and haven't. Stick to the case, not to the publicity about the case.

One point that *is* part of your job immediately that media become involved is to canvas with your counsel the formal parameters of media access to and presentation of facts about the case. Identity of the parties should normally be protected by court order if necessary, and you may have the right to apply for specific orders to govern media presence in court to the extent that this affects the case, particularly where kids need to take the witness stand. When the media arrive on a case, review these options in case it is necessary to pursue them.

KEEPING THE FAITH

Between the myths and stereotypes discussed in the first chapter, and the ambivalencies surrounding your job discussed in this one, you may be feeling a touch bothered about the feasibility of getting on with daily functioning!

Rest assured.

We'll move on straightaway to the nuts and bolts of handling the court process effectively. The subjects discussed so far are intended to help you develop a sense of the context in which your work is done, and to point out some of the sharp edges which are often only apparent when you walk right into them.

The purpose of referring to some of these edges at the outset is that when you notice where they are, you place yourself in a position to do something about them, even if only to avoid them. In many ways the legal system *is* a queer sort of place to have to try to protect kids. And your job is a strange sort of job, which exposes you to the ventilation of a whole range of big and little angsts about kids and families and what kind of society we live in.

To navigate the ship of your professional soul through such murky, troubled waters, you at least need to pinpoint some of the rocks and narrower channels. This task is not particularly complicated or mysterious. It takes an investment of enormous amounts of energy to maintain free-floating confusion about the undercurrent dynamics of testifying to protect kids. It takes only a modest amount of energy to build your own map of the shadowy landmarks. The map must be your own, but perhaps reading this far will have saved you a step or two.

Through the ongoing process of developing a sense of what your job is all about, you will need a source of strength to deal with some of the glitches and wrinkles of the system. That source of strength is already at hand. It lies in the magnificent choice you have made in the first place—to protect kids.

The glitches and wrinkles, particularly the ones that involve negativity directed at you, are ultimately easy to move through if you keep an eye on your reason for getting involved with protection work. You are a part of a beautiful mission. You have chosen to offer your energy to heal the pain of kids. When you bear in mind the vital importance of this work, it makes the momentary irritations of the crazier parts of the job easy to put up with. When lawyers and judges and parents get cranky with you, remember why you are there on the front line. Taking emotional bullets is no big deal, compared to the goal of protecting the child. The goal is important enough to enable you to put up with a lot.

Others more oriented to it can tinker with the system and speak the great truths about our kids in a way society can hear. Meanwhile, you are out there, trying to make a difference, one kid at a time.

Everything counts. Every kid counts. Every step you take that comforts a kid's pain or prevents it, counts. So what if nobody else wants to do it. So what if collectively society prefers not to think about it. The pain is real, the help helps, and it's not a perfect world. Your choice to do the work you do adds a bit more perfection, a bit more love, every day. That's worth putting up with a bit of harassment here and there, don't you think?

In a sense you are maidservant to the myth that we are a society that loves and honors its children. The truth to keep in the heart is that society wants to love and honor its children, but often doesn't. You do, and *that's not myth;* it's reality. And that's not just worth something. It's worth a lot.

So let's get on with the business of bringing love into the courtroom.

Without saying so, of course.

Chapter 3

TRIALS AND TRIBULATIONS: TAKING THE CASE TO COURT

REMOVAL OF THE CHILD FOR SERIOUS CAUSE

The act of removing a child from his home triggers the involvement of the legal system. Under what circumstances is the state justified in intervening in private family life by removing a child?

If you have no precise answer to this question, do not be discouraged. No one else has, either.

Protection statutes vary in the language they use to determine when a removal of a child is warranted. Some speak generally of "lack of proper parental care" or "abuse or neglect." Others attempt to be more specific, referring to "physical, mental or emotional" abuse, or listing elements of neglect, such as lack of adequate food, clothing, supervision, education, and medical care.

As a result, protection statutes are criticized for their vagueness and ambiguity. The terminology used begs the question rather than answering it. What *is* emotional abuse? What does "proper parental care" mean? How much supervision is "adequate?"

Practicing social workers need to be aware of the concern which lies behind the criticism. The concern is that unless the statutes can somehow spell out the details of every circumstance that justifies state intervention, social workers are left with so little guidance that they will apprehend casually.

If the statutes themselves are not very helpful in guiding your decision about whether to remove a child, what steps can you take to make sure the decision to remove is sound? Consider running the decision through the following protocol:

1. Is the Child Safe?

This is the most important question to answer. You are a trained social worker and you bring important intuitive skills to an assessment of whether the child is at risk. If you consider he is at risk, he should be removed, period.

The question is not whether you have sufficient legal evidence. This is something you can discuss with your counsel as a separate issue. The question is simply whether the child is safe at home. If he is not, he should be removed. That's your job. We can deal with the court side of the decision later.

2. Are There Emergency Circumstances?

All protection statutes provide for immediate removal of a child who is living in circumstances of a present danger. Make a detailed written summary of events as soon as possible after the incident, so that sensory images of the child's experience can be captured while they are fresh and vivid.

3. What Voluntary Help Has Been Offered?

Most family problems are adequately mitigated with offers of voluntary services. When this approach does not work, or no longer works, a point is reached where you have to consider removal of the child. Before making that decision, do an inventory of the services offered. *Were* all the needed services offered, such that the family could remain together? Were services offered reasonably, in a manner that improved the odds that they would be accepted by the parent? Were services refused arbitrarily, or for reasons that are understandable from the parents' point of view? How much energy was put into offering alternative services, or offering them in a different manner which might be acceptable to the parents?

In summary, what concrete efforts have been made to deal with family problems *short of* the removal of the child?

4. Have Sources Been Checked?

Where allegations of abuse or neglect have been received, they need to be investigated, of course. In some cases these reports may be the only initial information you have. How reliable or credible is the informant? How serious is the behavior reported? Have the parents been confronted with the allegation? Is their response appropriate?

For example, a report from a teacher that she observed the parent whack the child across the bum when the child was picked up from school is *not* enough, by itself, to justify intervention. Parents are entitled to discipline their children. Physical discipline, by itself, is not necessarily child abuse.

"Minor" allegations such as this justify investigation, perhaps, but not immediate intervention. The investigation may produce evidence of abuse or it may not. In some cases the allegations are so trivial that even an investigation may not be warranted. The slippery dividing line between serious and trivial situations can be hard to draw.

If you work in a jurisdiction that uses inexperienced workers to handle intake reports, but also insists that *every* allegation be "fully" investigated, you have a problem. There is only so much time and energy available. The volume of reports of child abuse and neglect escalate rapidly every year. The risk is that some agencies spend so much time investigating trivial reports that the serious cases do not get the energy they deserve.

The fear is that a child may be hurt if every report is not fully investigated. That fear is warranted, but the fact is that some kids are hurt or neglected or injured, no matter what. *The system cannot protect every single child.* In attempting to do just that, resources are often removed from the serious cases.

Make your *own* judgment about the validity of the allegations. Keep your job, and its limitations, in perspective. Child protection is not about making life happier for every single child. The state has no such mandate. The state *has* a mandate to intervene if a child is not safe.

How serious *is* the situation at hand? If you find yourself unable to answer this question quickly and clearly, it may well be that the situation is not serious enough to justify intervention.

5. Is the Intervention "Realistic?"

There is an element of hypocrisy in the formalities of the protection process. It is as if we pretend that there are only two categories of families, those who continuously love and honor their children, and those who abuse and neglect them.

Virtually every parent loses his temper with his child occasionally. We all have regrets about how we have treated our own children at one time or another. We are only human and we make mistakes. Parenting is a demanding job at the best of times. Good parents as well as bad parents often feel that they could have done better.

This is why opposing counsel will sometimes ask you on the witness stand about whether you have ever lost your temper with your own children, if you have any. Or whether you accept it as realistic that parents do lose their temper sometimes, if you don't have children. What opposing counsel is getting at is the core belief system you bring to your work. He knows that if he can establish that you believe that the only acceptable quality of parenting is that which abounds in nothing but unremitting love and caring, he can call your professional judgment into question. Minor lapses in good care are not a sufficiently serious peril for a child to be removed; they are part of ordinary family life everywhere.

Be aware of your attitudes on this point, and be prepared to explain them. When you wear the mantle of authority as an agency worker mandated to protect children, you are *not* mandated with carte blanche authority to do good wherever you think it needs to be done. You are there for the child who is at risk, whose care falls below the minimal standards (whatever *they* are!) to which every child is entitled. Families involved in curfew battles with teenagers, blended family conflicts, or turmoil arising from marital separation, do not warrant state intervention per se.

6. Have you Discussed Intervention with the Parents?

Except in emergency circumstances, your intention to remove a child should be discussed with the parents. Disclosure of your intention to remove is not only simple fairness to the parents. It also conveys how seriously you regard the situation, and may result in cooperation that has previously been absent. As such, discussion of the decision may have therapeutic value to the point that the intervention can be avoided.

If you have removed the child without prior disclosure of your intention, be prepared to explain and justify your approach. There are situations where there are good grounds for not discussing intervention ahead of time, such as those where the circumstances are so volatile that the discussion could well provoke violence or result in the family simply vanishing overnight. Be specific about how you have come to your decision.

7. Are the Required Resources Available?

The unspoken premise of state intervention is that the child will be better off in agency care. In the specific case, make an assessment about whether what *this* child needs is actually available. Resources are limited and there have been notorious cases in which kids have been saved from one form of harm at the hands of their parents, only to languish unserviced in state care, or even abused by their new caretakers.

The courts are more alert to the limitations of the system these days. They want to be assured that the *specific* services required for *this* child *can* be provided. In other words, you will need to be able to articulate a plan that convinces the court that the child will be *demonstrably* better off in care. Without this articulation of a viable plan, the court may consider that while things are far less than ideal at home, the child is better off remaining there.

DRY RUNS BEFORE COURT

Presenting intervention facts effectively the first time round depends on checking a few things out before you go to court. Even if the initial court appearance on a protection case is a brief one, your presentation will benefit from consideration of the following suggestions:

1. Have You Put Your Concerns in Writing?

As mentioned earlier, the foundation question is whether you consider the child to be at risk. If he is, reduce your concerns to a paragraph of writing. Words are your main tool in court. You need to be able to articulate the risk, to flesh it out in sensory images that make the child's situation real in the mind of the judge.

Read your paragraph over as a disinterested party. Would the words alone convince you of the risk, if you were not involved in the case?

2. Have You Rehearsed the Presentation of the Facts?

Using your writing as the guideline, speak the case out loud. Then put the written material away and speak the case out loud without notes. Give yourself a two minute limit. Within that time, can you cover all the bases? Do you say who's who in the family constellation? Can you describe the family situation in a single sentence, or two? Can you articulate the risk in one sentence, period? Are there irrelevant details included which muddy the point? Is your language confined to clear, specific details and sensory images? Have you used formalistic language ("the mother indicated to me" vs. "the mother told me"), jargon ("the mother was ambivalent about her son" vs. "the mother said she couldn't stand having her son in the house"), subjective language ("the mother was under obvious stress" vs. "the mother's hands shook, her eyes kept darting back and forth, and she was unable to finish her sentences"), opinion ("the mother was drunk" vs. "her speech was slurred, her eyes were bloodshot, and she stumbled twice against the couch") or mushy language implying uncertainty ("it seemed to me," "I felt," "she appeared to have").

Social workers, like many witnesses, have a tendency to dress up their language when they testify in court. The court system has enough dramatic elements built into it already. Choose not to see yourself on a stage. Just tell the story.

3. Have You Tested Your Presentation?

Collar a co-worker and tell the story. Is it convincing? Is it clear? Get feedback. Note especially any supplementary questions your friend asks. Could you have addressed these in your presentation itself? Ideally, you will have addressed everything that needs to be addressed, so no further questions need to be asked. Getting feedback from a colleague is the best way to check how complete your presentation is.

4. Have You Played Devil's Advocate?

Again with a co-worker, attack your presentation from the perspective of parents' counsel. Take the role of challenger or defender, whichever is most comfortable. If you play the challenger, use your powers of empathy to identify with the role of opposing counsel. What gaps or weaknesses appear? Where are the best places in the presentation to probe for facts suggesting that the action taken was not reasonable or justified? What lines of attack would be most fruitful, if *you* were on the attack?

If you play defender, be prepared to concede error calmly and easily. Keep the focus on the child. Acknowledge limitations. Give credit to the parents where possible.

Notice how easy or difficult it was to challenge your presentation. The task in court is not damage control, to protect yourself from attack. The task in court is to do well enough in the presentation itself that a clear, concrete picture of events is presented convincingly enough that the attack component is minimized as a result.

5. Have You Briefed Your Counsel?

Give your counsel the same presentation, even by telephone. The purpose of briefing your counsel is to orient him to the case, but the secondary benefit is comment he may offer by way of response. Notice the supplementary questions he asks and consider whether to revise your presentation to anticipate these.

A further purpose of briefing your counsel is to get his opinion of the evidence you have. It is your role to remove a child who is at risk, and that decision is yours alone. It is your counsel's role to advise you as to whether your presentation includes sufficient convincing evidence to persuade the court.

If there are real problems with your presentation from an evidentiary point of view, you will need to rethink your presentation. Your counsel may not make suggestions as to how you approach presenting the evidence unless you ask him. So ask him.

As you gain experience in presenting cases to court, notice the judge's comments about your own presentations and those of your colleagues. Every good trial lawyer plays close attention to comments from the bench, in hopes of sensing which way the judicial winds are blowing. You are interested in this aspect as well, but besides hinting at the result, judicial responses to your testimony are the best guide to the court's expectations of you on the stand.

Notice which kinds of interventions the judge seems to feel are very solid, and which he considers loose. What is the judicial attitude to physical discipline within a family? What kinds of parenting are seen as marginal rather than outright neglectful? What preliminary attempts at service are expected prior to an intervention?

In the protection field it is a cliche to say that each case is decided on its facts. As mentioned, there is very little "law" involved. Protection statutes are perhaps necessarily vague about what specifically constitutes neglect or abuse. What you are left with is an enormous discretion to intervene. The discretion is tempered by accountability in court, where the edges of protection concepts are defined for the particular case by the particular judge. These may be your best working guides, so comments should be noted.

You, too, are in court for the particular case. But each case offers the opportunity to hone your presentation of the next one. If this opportunity is ignored, you may find yourself inventing the wheel over and over again, and running into the same problems repeatedly. The answers to most of these problems are available in court. You need to choose to see them, though, or they remain invisible.

DOUBLE BIND: TRUST BETRAYED

The court aspect of being a protection social worker creates a special double bind. As social worker *qua* social worker, you strive to develop a trusting relationship with those you wish to help. You know that trust is an important factor affecting how influential you can be and how readily offered help is accepted.

If the child is ultimately removed from the home, you take on the professional witness part of your role. In this capacity you are expected to tell the full story of the family, including facts which the family may have come to believe you no longer consider serious issues. Or the family, having taken you into their confidence, may feel betrayed to find you in open court, spilling the beans and airing their dirty laundry.

Intervention and court proceedings can seriously damage your ongoing therapeutic relationship with the family, but it need not. What is needed to neutralize the sense of betrayal is specific action ahead of time.

Parents need to know from the beginning of your involvement that it is part of your job to testify in court about neglect and abuse cases. They need to be told that what they tell you is confidential, but only so long as there is no legal proceeding. If removal of the child is imminent, you need to sit down with the parents and let them know what you will be discussing in court, as part of your job.

This is particularly important when your application to court is with the consent of the parents, or at least is unopposed by them. Having agreed to a course of action aimed at resolving problems from this point forward, parents are understandably surprised to hear you testify about the past situation as a foundation for the plan. Explain ahead of time that you are required to do this, so there is no surprise.

In most cases the quality of the working relationship between yourself and the parents *after* court is a direct function of your taking the time to prepare them for your testimony *before* court. Usually parents can accept this aspect of your job if it is explained to them ahead of time. Trying to explain things after the fact is often unsuccessful; too much goodwill has been lost and the working relationship may be burdened by a return to its mistrustful beginnings.

RESCUER AND PERSECUTOR

There is an ulterior quality to the relationship between the social worker and the parent which sometimes becomes visible when the legal process is invoked by removal of the child. Examining the dynamic at work can make it easier to understand the impact of the legal process on the family problems which have brought you to court in the first place. For a fuller description of rescuer-persecutor dynamics, see Claude Steiner's brilliant work, *Scripts People Live,* from which many of the following ideas are drawn.

Members of the helping professions are classic rescuers, there to provide needed assistance. The wrench in the works is that social workers, unlike other classic rescuers such as firefighters or police officers, give help to recipients who are more often resistant to help than grateful. In fact, the more serious the family problem, the more likely it is that resistance will take its ultimate form—denial that a problem exists at all.

It is easier to observe the dynamic if the elements in the relationship are exaggerated, perhaps to the point of caricature. Let's say that in your dealings with the family, you offer to help with the problems at hand. The offer of help is framed as power-neutral; that is, you do not refer openly to the fact that you have the ultimate power to remove the child if necessary. In turn, the parent pretends to believe that your offer of help is power-neutral. You wish to be regarded as a friend, so the parent pretends to treat you that way.

Of course, you and the parent both know that you are not a personal friend, but that this is your job, that you are paid to be there, and that behind your professional friendship stands the full force and authority of the state, including, ultimately, the legal system. Your presence is also a critical point in the life of the parent, who knows that change in lifestyle is going to be discussed and that the decision to change is going to be presented as a voluntary choice. As the power-differential is unacknowledged, the parent may go along and pretend to make changes voluntarily, while experiencing these choices as involuntary.

By this point the stage is set for both of you to play the game of Rescuer and Victim. (True rescuers, as mentioned, are power neutral; true victims do not contribute to their own oppression. To be characterized as a game, the Rescuer must see herself as one-up and the Victim must see herself as one-down.) The essence of the game from the perspective of the Rescuer is that the real object is to remain in the position of Rescuer, which means that the "problem" must not be solved, as this would terminate the role. The essence of the game from the perspective of the Victim is to maintain the Victim stance, which similarly means that the problem must not be solved. Secretly, the Victim sees the Rescuer as a Persecutor.

The best example of the Rescuer-Victim game is that of the alcoholic and the "helping" spouse. So long as the alcoholic can rely on the spouse to bail him out and make excuses for him (to "rescue" him), he can go on drinking.

When the game is played in a protection case, a crunch-point arrives with the realization that the help offered is not actually helping. The Victim parent will make efforts, but sabotages them one way or another, and they come to naught. By this strategy the Victim has reversed the power-differential. The Victim has regained "control" in the relationship and is now one-up: "you can't help me."

At this point the Rescuer is obliged to shift roles and become the Persecutor, blaming the Victim for sabotaging the Rescue. Secretly the Victim enjoys the pay-off of being blamed, as she has seen the Rescuer as a Persecutor from the beginning. She then returns to a one-down position, which she is more used to anyway.

The hidden purpose of this game is to play out the three roles and to shift back and forth between one-up and one-down positions. The game is ruined if the "problem" is solved, so it is not solved.

In a protection case prior to any legal proceeding, one clue to the presence of this dynamic occurs if the parent Victim shifts to the Persecutor role. This involves calls to the social worker's supervisor, asking for a new social worker. The parent becomes one-up by identifying the social worker as the "real" problem: "My difficulties would be solved if I just had a different social worker." If a new social worker is assigned, the decision to do this sustains the game, which is then repeated with the new social worker.

The courtroom version of the game is evident when the Persecutor parent blames the problem on the social worker. Every action of the social worker is called into question, her real motivations are questioned, personal bias is alleged.

The Victim-Rescuer-Persecutor game is observable in many situations. Families who are well-trained in it can play it for years. Lawyers who play it tell their clients what to do instead of advising them. Psychiatrists who play it have patients who do not improve. Teachers who play it have students who remain learning-disabled. Social workers who play it have clients who never solve their problems.

The two clues to the presence of the game are that the stated purpose of the relationship (solving the "problem") never gets accomplished, and that the power-differential is maintained (the roles may alter, but at each point one party is one-up and other one-down). A lack of positive change alone is not proof of the presence of the game, however. Many factors make it difficult for people to choose to change their lives. An absence of any progress at all warrants checking out whether the game is being played.

The prerequisite for the game to be played is a Victim existential position ("I can't change") and a Rescuer existential position ("I can't really help people and people can't really help themselves"). Proof that the game is present occurs when either party moves into the Persecutor role. The Rescuer does this by getting angry and blaming the Victim; the Victim does this by getting angry and blaming the Rescuer.

Prior to court proceedings the only way to neutralize the game is not to play any of the roles. Returning to the example of the alcoholic version, this occurs when the spouse refuses to Rescue or Persecute, so the Victim must either take responsibility for his own problem, or find a new

Rescuer/Persecutor. In a protection case the game is neutralized when the social worker consistently treats the parent as empowered to make changes and responsible for the consequences of her own choices (power-parity). Help (I'll help *you* to do) is offered, and Rescue (I'll do this *for* you) is refused.

When the game is initiated in court, the parent will take the Persecutor role and attempt to shift the focus of the proceeding to the personal and professional deficits of the social worker. There is risk attached to spending time defending the social worker in these circumstances. By doing so, the court is co-opted into the game and the persecution is successful, in the sense that the focus is on the social worker instead of the child.

Be aware of this dynamic when you take a protection case to court. It can explain why your counsel may not be too energetic in defending you against parental allegations. If your actual conduct is seriously called into question, of course, this must be addressed. But if it is merely the game at play, it is often just as well to allow the parent to have her say without response. None of the players in the legal system will likely articulate the dynamics of the game, but judges and protection lawyers are just as aware of how and why "let's blame the social worker" is played in court as you are of how and why "if only I could get a new social worker" is played outside of court.

Mention must be made of a special variation of the Victim stance which is sometimes seen in protection court. Normally it is far preferable to negotiate a mutually-agreed solution out of court, or as a basis for a consent order. Sometimes negotiations are fruitless for no apparent reason, and a contested case proceeds with a sense of inevitability about it. Parents who are very wedded to a Victim stance may secretly insist on their day in court precisely to expose and be rebuked for the dirty laundry which most people would prefer to be dealt with more discreetly. Nothing will do, but that the whole sad story, complete with a parade of witnesses, be told in a public courtroom. When you have this type of case, you need to cut your losses early and conserve the energy you might otherwise invest in negotiating an arrangement by consent. The only thing for it is to get on with the trial.

An even more rare variation is the case in which the Victim parent insists on the trial and sits through it unemotionally. In one example of this, the mother sat quietly through a four-day trial, making notes. As the evidence seemed overwhelming, both the social worker and her counsel became overconfident and there were gaps in the evidence.

When the mother's turn came to present her evidence, she filled in the gaps with evidence in her favor that was too late to refute. She won the case, and the children were ordered returned to her. The proof that she was playing the Victim game (in the "I'm going to get the social worker" Persecutor mode) came the day after the trial concluded, when she signed consents to the children becoming permanent wards and adopted. She had "won."

This section is not intended to imply that psychological games are inevitable for social workers, that all social workers play Rescuer, or that all parents play Victim. However the helping role *is* susceptible to this particular dynamic with some parents, and when it occurs, it tends to slop over into the court proceeding. Every case has its own dynamics, and it is worth checking for clues to the presence of this one since it requires forms of handling that appear to be the opposite of what you might otherwise expect.

COURT: NEW GAME, NEW RULES

Under most protection statutes your first appearance in court takes place for the purpose of obtaining a court order permitting you to remove a child, or for the purpose of explaining the reasons for removal very shortly after the child has been removed. Under either procedure the first appearance tends to be short, with many other applications being heard in the same morning or afternoon. This "interim hearing" is distinguished from the "full hearing" some weeks or even months later, when you are expected to prove that the child was in need of protection on the basis of an investigation that has been completed over the intervening period.

At the interim hearing stage the court is asked to decide whether the child should stay in your care until the full hearing. To assist the court at this initial stage of the legal proceeding, either before or after the child has been removed from the family, you will likely have to prepare a written report of the circumstances.

The legal system prefers a linear (chronological), orderly, concise presentation of the relevant facts. You need to achieve a balance between disclosing enough concrete, specific detail to make the child's situation real in the mind of the judge, and giving general information about the family situation without getting swept away in side issues.

Writing reports for the court is, like all the other aspects of your court work, a *learnable skill.* By reviewing the reports of your colleagues you can get a sense of who has a natural flair for the task and who is seasoned in it. To avoid inventing the wheel each time, notice the aspects of the task you have trouble with and those that come easily. Watch for the uses of language and other techniques of others that you can adopt as your own. Watch the evolution of your own skills; notice whether the task becomes easier as you go on and gain experience with it.

At the first appearance in court you will likely be required to summarize the situation by testifying on the stand. To prepare for this, consider testifying to yourself, practicing on your own. Impose an arbitrary time limit on yourself: can you present a concise verbal picture in sixty seconds or two minutes? Have you covered all the bases?

Notice what happens to your personal sense of power as you approach the time of testifying in court. How much power do you choose to give away to anxiety? If you do experience anxiety, which is perfectly normal, do you choose to do anything about it? Some of the techniques available to deal with the jitters have already been discussed:

1. a brief relaxation meditation before court;
2. vigorous physical exercise;
3. observing in court ahead of time;
4. visiting the courtroom when it is empty and getting comfortable with it;
5. subjecting yourself to questioning by a friend or colleague;
6. asking your lawyer to rehearse your testimony with you.

Have you made a specific request to your lawyer about what form of questioning you would prefer? You will be more effective and credible if you are simply asked to explain the situation and do so on your own, but you can be led through your testimony step-by-step if you tell your lawyer that this is what you want. Instruct your lawyer to make a practice at the end of your testimony of asking you whether there is anything further you want to add. This technique is sometimes just the little push that is needed to bring to the fore some point that you *and* your lawyer might otherwise miss.

Some social workers have a natural flair for relaxed, clear, concise articulation of events on the witness stand. *Ask* them what techniques they use to achieve this. Some may not be conscious of exactly how they go about it. Others will have concrete strategies, which they will be happy to share with you. Many good witnesses have a clear mental image of the sequence of events, to which they refer internally while they are testifying.

Notice which sensory mode is your personal favorite. Visual people can present a chronology of events more easily if they have prepared a rough flow chart on paper ahead of time, to which they mentally refer later. Auditory people need to practice telling the story out loud; the oral sequence is easier for them to recall. Kinesthetic people may prefer to practice their testimony with someone else, "as if" on the witness stand, so that the whole experience of formally telling the story can be recalled.

New social workers are sometimes so involved with the family situation that they get lost in detail when they first testify in court. Effective testimony takes into account that the other players in court know little or nothing about the case. The lawyers and the judge have a natural human curiosity to know about what is going on, but the testimony must focus on the specific circumstances that warrant the child's removal.

Unless there is serious dispute at this initial stage, your testimony will take only a very few minutes. A common beginning is to state how long you have been involved with the family. Next, give the judge a sense of who's who. Where does the child before the court fit into the family constellation in relation to the number and ages of his siblings? What is the marital status of the parents? Is the child living with one or both of his natural parents? Are there stepparents or common law spouses involved?

Next, describe the specific, concrete events that you consider warrant the child's removal. Take special care with your language here. A poor description will muffle the reality of the child's risk in the home. Then tell the court what your immediate plan would be if the child is to remain in care, and take a clear position about what type of access between the child and the parents you feel is appropriate.

The period during which you are on the stand and asked questions by your own counsel is called *examination-in-chief.* During this time your counsel cannot ask leading questions. This means he can ask, "What happened on the evening of May 17th?" but he cannot ask, "Was there a problem with babysitting arrangements on the evening of May 17th?" A leading question is one in which the answer is suggested in the form of the question. The restriction against leading questions means that your counsel has a limited ability to ask about the points that need to be addressed. You need to know what they are before you go on the stand.

Sometimes there will be opposing counsel at the initial stage, who will conduct a *cross-examination.* Under cross-examination leading questions *can* be asked. For example, opposing counsel can ask, "Overall wouldn't you say that the mother made reasonable babysitting arrangements?" Leading questions are often framed this way, inviting a yes or no answer without elaboration.

Coping effectively with cross-examination is the greatest concern of social workers who testify in court. As the interim hearing often does not involve cross-examination, the topic will not be dealt with further here. For information about techniques available to deal with cross-examination, see Chapters 4 and 10.

Your first appearance in court is an opportunity to demonstrate your awareness of the rule against hearsay. How you handle hearsay information can mean the difference between whether the court regards you as a competent professional witness or not, since the rule is basic to all testimony of witnesses in court. The general rule is that you cannot quote the statements of third parties in your own testimony. You are confined to telling the court your own direct observations of events.

For example, if you begin a portion of your testimony with the statement, "The school counsellor telephoned and told me . . . ," opposing counsel will object on the basis that you are about to cite hearsay information. It is immediately apparent to the court that you are either unaware of the rule against hearsay, or careless about it. First impressions tend to last; this is not the first impression you want to make as a professional witness.

On the other hand, it is perfectly acceptable to say, "The school counsellor telephoned me and as a result of the discussion I visited the home." You can then proceed to state your observations in the home. There is nothing wrong with stating that the school counsellor called. This is a fact. It is when you move on to quote statements made to you that you violate the rule against hearsay.

Hearsay is dealt with in detail in Chapter 12. For the purpose of dealing with the issue at the interim hearing stage, only three further points need to be made.

First, the practice in some courts is to relax the rule against hearsay at the interim hearing stage. The rationale is that as this stage in the court process is preliminary to the full hearing, the court may need to hear information which is not properly acceptable at trial in order to get a complete picture of what is going on in the family. The other aspect of the rationale is that protection cases are sometimes seen as more in the nature of an inquiry or investigation than an adversarial trial. The purpose is not so much a "contest" between the parents and the state as simply to find out whether the child is at risk.

If your court has adopted this more informal approach, you would still be wise to avoid hearsay. You will always appear more professional as a witness if you stick to your own observations rather than quote the statements made by parties who are not present in court and available for cross-examination. Indeed, your job is to *verify* the risk to the child through your own investigation, not to *assume* the risk because of what someone else has said.

Second, like most rules created by the legal system, there are exceptions. The major one in the context of protection cases is the exception that says that you *can* quote the statements made to you by *parties* to the proceeding. For practical purposes, this means you can quote what the parents told you, but no one else. The rationale is that if a party to a legal proceeding says something contrary to his or her interest, it is more likely to be reliable.

So while you can't quote what the school counsellor told you in the earlier example, you can say, "As a result of a telephone call from the school counsellor, I discussed the call with the mother, and she said . . ." Routing third party statements back to the parents and quoting their responses is an important evidence-collecting skill.

Third, opposing counsel in protection cases are notable for being more ready to object to hearsay at the beginning of your evidence than later on. If you start right off quoting hearsay, you will certainly provoke objections. If you are obviously careful from the outset, later hearsay may get by without provoking objection from opposing counsel or comment from the judge.

Observing the rule from the beginning enhances your credibility and reliability. But do not be misled if the rule seems to be relaxed as you go on. The judge has an exceedingly clear sense of what constitutes hearsay. He may not interrupt your testimony when you violate the rule, but he may very well disregard all of the hearsay when he makes his decision.

There have been cases in which the social worker and her counsel have become confident about the result because the court appears to accept endless hearsay, only to have the judge make his decision by saying, "I have heard only hearsay evidence in this case, and as such evidence is not a proper basis for a protection order, I direct that the child be returned to the parents forthwith."

LEAVING YOUR TOOLBAG ON THE COURTHOUSE STEPS

Effective social work involves a whole toolbag of skills which enable the worker to pursue the task at hand without being diverted by dramas and crises. The irony is that while many of these skills are directly applicable to the court side of the social work job, some workers drop the entire toolbag on the courthouse steps.

Certainly court is a new game with new rules. This is no basis for choosing the stance of helplessness and disempowerment. The reason this sometimes occurs is due to seeing the obstacles in court process as fundamentally different from the obstacles to dealing effectively with people outside court.

The best example of this is the issue of coping with hostile cross-examination. Outside court every social worker is confronted frequently by the hostility of parents. Hostility goes with the work. A social worker does not waste time taking such hostility personally. She knows that the causes of it have little to do with her personally. The causes have to do with conflicts already present in the parent's life.

So the hostility is observed; made a note of, perhaps, but not permitted to enter the personal boundary. The social worker knows that if she becomes defensive or treats the hostility as personal rejection, she loses her effectiveness. The problem at hand will become invisible if the communication is diverted to focus on the red herring of personal justification in the face of hostility.

The same social worker may choose to turn to Jello® if opposing counsel becomes, or *appears* to become, hostile. Harsh questions, personal questions, unfair questions, aggressive questions; all are regarded as a basis for hurt feelings and self-justifying statements or anger.

These are, of course, precisely the responses which are sought to be provoked. In a severe case, they enable opposing counsel to *then* portray the worker as subject to emotionalism, overreaction, oversensitivity, and defensiveness. "How, Your Honor, can my clients expect calm and fair treatment at the hands of a social worker who is so quick to get emotionally upset at any questioning of her actions? And if this worker gets defensive so easily here, in the formality of a court of law, imagine the impact of her 'help' outside of court, where she is completely unrestrained?"

Observe police officer testimony by comparison. Like social workers, police officers are exposed to gratuitous hostility due to the nature of the job. In court police officers will be subject to aggressive cross-examination.

The effective police officer deals with hostility in court the same way she deals with it outside. The presence of the hostility is observed, but the matter at hand is addressed objectively, without "buying into" the hostility. The police officer's toolbag is brought *into* court, where it is just as useful as it is on the outside.

The vast majority of protection cases do not involve harsh cross-examination, but the example is still a good one to demonstrate the phenomenon of skills abandoned on the courthouse steps. Other skills include taking the time you need to respond appropriately (choosing not to be rushed), not agreeing to statements you really don't agree with (choosing not to be pushed), and declining to be diverted from the task at hand (maintaining the focus on the child).

In fact an inventory of your social work skills will show that most or all of them have a direct application in court. Noticing *how* they can be used in court is the first step to bringing the full toolbag of skills *with you* to the witness stand.

Clues to the possibility that you may be abandoning your own skills are internal thought processes on the theme of the question, "Who will protect me?" Will my counsel make sure everything is safe? Will the judge prevent unfair questions? Will *someone* guarantee that nothing irritating or upsetting will happen?

No one offers such guarantees in court anymore than anyone offers them outside. As with maintaining your cool in the field, maintaining your cool in court is up to you. You just need to *choose* to do it, with the skills already at hand.

Chapter 4

SELF–ASSESSMENT:
COURT SKILLS, COURT HABITS

AWARENESS AND ABILITY

Emotional reactions to the court process create a tendency for social workers to discount their own skills when they go to court. Some social workers abandon their whole toolbag of skills on the courthouse steps. The purpose of this chapter is to suggest mechanisms which can help to identify your skills and to clarify how they can assist you in court, with the goal of maintaining a conscious inventory of court habits which you can bring to bear on every protection case.

To make maximum use of these suggestions, consider setting aside any emotional reactions to court for a moment. If you operate on the premise that court skills are fundamentally different from other social worker skills, put this premise on the shelf as well. You can always pick it up again, if you wish, after you have finished this chapter.

As a substitute for disempowering approaches to assessing the skills needed for effective court work, consider the following alternative premises:

1. Effective court presentation involves *identifiable, learnable skills;* it is not a question of native talent.
2. As a professional social worker, you already possess the skills you need for court; it is a question of *seeing* how those skills apply in that forum and *using* them there.
3. Your effectiveness in a particular case depends far more on the court habits you bring to bear on *every* case than on the skills you use for the *particular* case.

There are a number of techniques you can use for self-assessment of your court skills. Have a look through the following exercises and try the ones that suit you best.

53

Exercise 1: The Inventory

Divide several blank sheets of paper in half so you have a left side and a right side. On the left side, brainstorm all the social worker skills that you can think of which you apply in the field every day. Don't bother with making your list orderly, just put everything down as it comes to you.

When you have finished, read your list over. You may be surprised at the wide variety of skills, small and large, that you use every day. This list comprises your *conscious* skills; that is, the ones you are readily aware of.

Next, give yourself a few minutes to reflect on feedback you have received about your work. You deal with a wide variety of people in your job and many of them will have commented on your work. Note on paper as many of the comments you can recall. This list comprises your *unconscious* skills; that is, the ones you apply to the task at hand so automatically that you are not readily aware of them. Some of these skills may be ones that you simply assume everyone has, so you may have discounted the feedback you have received. This assumption is probably wrong. What is second nature to one person is frequently a major challenge for another. Give yourself full credit for the skills you have that you don't even notice unless someone remarks on them.

Finally, review your two lists and note on the right-hand side how each of the skills is applicable in court. For example, the skill of not buying in to gratuitous hostility has been referred to earlier as a standard, necessary social worker skill that has direct applicability to the cross-examination component of court process.

When you are finished you may be surprised at the size of the inventory of court skills you already possess. Most social worker skills can be used in court in one situation or another. Give yourself full credit for identifying the skills you have that are available to bring along to court if you wish.

At a minimum this exercise should assist you in seeing that you are *not* starting from scratch when you go to court.

Exercise 2: Ranking Your Skills

What are the aspects of your work that you enjoy the most? These will often be things that you are particularly good at. Perhaps you enjoy meeting with your clients and assisting them to acknowledge what the problems are. Being clear about what the problems are is a court skill as well.

Perhaps you enjoy giving your clients the opportunity to ventilate their feelings. Allowing the players in the court process to ventilate their concerns without getting defensive is really the same skill applied in a different setting.

After identifying your favorite skills, reframe them to apply in the courtroom. If you do what you most enjoy in court as well as outside, you have identified your special talents in the courtroom. Give yourself credit.

With this exercise you will also have identified the skills you can offer to your colleagues. Situations which allow you to flourish may petrify others. Share what you can do.

Notice which tasks your colleagues seem to enjoy the most. This is a way of identifying resources that can be offered to you by others, if you ask. Take the time to observe senior workers in court. Take the opportunity to ask them afterwards about court skills that seem to come so easily to them. How did they achieve the particular skill? Finding out how they invented the wheel can save you from having to invent it entirely on your own.

The parts of your job that you have ranked as your least favorite probably have a courtroom version as well. Do you especially dislike being put on the spot and being asked pointed questions? If this bothers you in the field, it will bother you more in court. Identifying your least favorite skills is a way of confronting yourself with the areas that you can work on, if you choose.

Exercise 3: Conscious Skill Development

Some skills, like learning to walk, evolve unconsciously. Most adult skills require deliberate choice. When you learned to drive a car, you had to make the *decision* to develop the competence, you had to *identify* the separate skill components involved, you had to *practice*, and you had to *monitor* how well you were doing so that you could *adjust* your performance to suit the needs of different driving situations.

Developing competent court skills proceeds in the same way: you have to *decide* to improve your skills, *identify* what they are, *practice* the use of them, *monitor* how you're doing, and *adjust* to the needs of the particular case.

This requires a conscious choice to put the matter of court skills on your own professional agenda. Doing so pays off, but it does require an investment of energy. If court makes you nervous, notice how much energy you already invest in coping with anxiety. You can choose to take this same energy and invest it in skill development, if you wish.

Notice thoughts running through your head that say, "I can't do it," "It's too difficult for me," or "It's all impossible." These are just forms of resistance. You can notice these thoughts, acknowledge them, and move through them if you wish. *Notice* whether you *choose* to take responsibility for your own skill development, or if you *choose* to stay with resistance. It isn't necessary to judge your own choice. But you do need to *own* the choice, in order to retain your power to decide. Be gentle with yourself. You are responsible for the consequences of your choices whatever they are, but you need not expect that you will take on every challenge and assume every risk. You get to choose what you want to work on and what you don't.

Exercise 4: Changing What You Can Change

If presenting protection cases in court seems complicated and difficult, try breaking the task down by noting what you can control and what you can't.

Some parts of court process are wholly out of your hands and subject to external control. Which parts are these? How difficult do you find them? Some social workers spend a lot of energy being irritated about parts of the system they can do absolutely nothing about. Once these parts are identified, the issue can be reframed: what we can change, we can change; what we can't, we need to accept. Choose to come to better terms of acceptance of the parts you have no power to change. Remaining stuck in negativity is not only a choice, it is one which requires enormous energy to maintain.

All the parts of the court process which are not controlled externally lie within your own control.

Each of *these* parts can be changed in one of two ways. Some, such as how you communicate with your counsel, how you prepare your case notes, how you get ready to testify, and how you respond to questions on the witness stand, can be changed by choices you make in your *exterior* life. In effect, you can change your own environment by changing how you handle yourself and your tasks. You can be open with your counsel about what you want and what you need. You can review your casenotes by noticing what is provable evidence and what is not *as you go along*, instead of finding out in court.

The other way to change the parts that you find difficult are through choices you make in your *interior* life. What happens inside of us often *feels* as if it is happening "*to* us." In fact, our feelings are really choices too.

If you find court work stressful, chances are that a lot of the stress is due to the choice of reacting rather than responding. To react ("to act again; to repeat") means buying whatever is offered on the outside, swallowing it whole, and replicating the stress factor inside. To respond ("to answer; to reply") means acknowledging what is happening on the outside, taking in the parts that are safe, and *choosing* what "answer" to give to the stimulus.

How you feel about court process is a matter of choice. By seeing your interior life as based on the choice to respond, you not only create alternative experiences in the process, but you reclaim the power and energy that is otherwise given over to reacting, to "eating" the negativities that are offered for consumption. You don't have to eat what is put on your plate. You can eat what you want and leave the rest.

Review your concerns about court process from this perspective of change and control. For all the limitations that you can't do anything about, there is a large territory remaining that you can alter directly or choose to handle differently internally. Notice that the validity of this statement is probably already familiar to you regarding your work in the field. If it is valid there, why not apply it in court?

The feelings of powerlessness and intimidation that some social workers feel about going to court are perfectly understandable. As discussed earlier, the system is designed in many respects to produce just these sorts of reactions. The way to transcend the reactions lies in becoming aware of the skills involved in court, noticing how skills used outside court work just as well inside, acknowledging strengths and weaknesses, and making skill development in court a conscious part of your professionalism.

Every time you go to court you have an opportunity to enhance your power and your skills. Every time you prepare for court you have an opportunity to try out a new approach to a problem that has beleaguered you in the past. There is no magic prescription, but throughout this book a variety of skills, tactics, and techniques will be discussed. With each one you have the opportunity to assess yourself and add to the toolbag you bring to court.

STATE AND PARENT: THE POWER DIFFERENTIAL

There is a huge difference between the resources available to you and your agency, and those available to the parents you work with.

Is this power differential relevant to presenting a protection case in court?

Not directly. The legal issue in the courtroom is whether the child was at risk to the point that his removal was justified.

However, everyone involved in the court case is aware of the practical difference in power, and you should be as well. To oversimplify only slightly, the same factors which put the parent at a disadvantage in trying to care properly for the child operate to put the parent at a disadvantage in trying to persuade the judge to order the return of the child.

Occasionally the power differential is seen in starkest terms by parents' counsel, or even the judge. You, after all, represent the government, with all its apparently limitless resources. The parents' primary problem is often poverty, which aggravates all the normal stresses and strains of raising a family. Parents cannot normally afford private counsel in a court case, nor can they afford to hire experts to contradict your experts.

Maintaining an awareness of the power differential is a specific court skill. A protection case is not a private lawsuit between individual persons. It is an inquiry into allegations raised by the state (you) against a private individual. Because of this, you need to be sensitive to the side effects of the power differential:

1. Endless Resources

If opposing counsel or the judge appear to imply that you have endless resources to assist the family, you need to be prepared to address the issue of limitations to the help you and your agency can offer. This has to do with explaining the difference between what is preferable and what is possible.

You need not apologize for the limitations of what you can do, or try to avoid the issue. Tackle it head on. It is easy for people outside government systems to develop unrealistic notions of the staffing and funding available. You can agree that a particular service or course of action would be desirable at the same time that you explain the concrete reasons why it is not an available option. Being seen as comfortable in acknowledging the limitations of the service you can provide enhances credibility. It also ensures that you don't agree to a plan that just won't work because you don't have the resources to service it.

2. Adversarialness

In a legal contest between equals, each party is seen as having an equal opportunity to make the best of his case. When the "contest" is between a state agency and a private individual, the balance of equality is shifted to the point that special care needs to be taken to neutralize the adversarial component of a legal case wherever possible.

You are not in court to "win" the case. Nor should you be seen as seeking to win. After all, you are not in court to add to your caseload. There is no quota system for state wards.

You are in court to present *all* of the evidence about the child's situation. This includes all the positive evidence you have about the parenting abilities being investigated. Because you have greater resources to present your "side" of a legal case, you must not only be fair, but be seen to be fair. Your presentation of the facts needs to be evenhanded, giving credit where due, but essentially neutral.

Under the circumstances parents will generally be forgiven expressions of anger, resentment, and resistance. Who would not react with such emotions to a state intervention to remove a child?

Similar expressions of frustration on your part, however, will damage your credibility. You are subject to a higher expectation of self-control in your presentation.

3. Accountability

The act of removal of a child from his family implies that you consider the risk involved to justify the parents being held formally accountable for their actions. Keeping parents accountable for the protection of their own children is central to your job.

The resultant case in court is the mechanism created to make you accountable in turn. You *do* have broad discretion and substantial resources, but you are expected to account openly, in a court of law, for your intrusion into private family affairs.

This balancing of discretionary state intervention with accountability in court is intended to mitigate the power differential between the state and the parents. The legal onus is on you to justify the intervention, not on the parents to prove the intervention was unnecessary.

4. Higher Evidentiary Expectations

Everyone in the courtroom knows that you are a professional notetaker, a professional witness. The parents may live a hurly-burly, catch-as-catch-can lifestyle, and it is understood that after a home visit they get on with their lives while you go back to the office to make a written record of the events observed.

When the parent testifies, failures of memory, vagueness, and a lack of orderliness of the story are tolerated far more by the court than when you take the witness stand. If your counsel points out contradictions in the parent's story, the judge will be less concerned than if similar contradictions are pointed out in your own evidence.

Errors in remembering are normal for everyone. An apparent memory error by a parent will possibly affect credibility, but allowance is made for the fact that people do not live their lives in anticipation of retelling the facts in court. You *are* seen as living your professional life preparing for court, and your testimony requires meticulousness in order for you to remain credible. Ordinary witnesses are expected to backtrack or waffle a bit if they are caught out in a contradiction. *You* are expected to be clear about what you know and what you don't know, and to readily acknowledge error when it is pointed out to you.

POWER PLAYS BEFORE COURT

Power plays, as Claude Steiner defines them in his book, *The Other Side of Power,* have to do with specific techniques used to obtain something from someone against that person's will.

You will be familiar with numerous power plays used by some parents. Passive power plays include forgetting appointments, not following through, not returning calls. These devices enable the person using them to retain control, to avoid doing what is being requested.

In discussion with parents and their counsel prior to court, be wary of the presence of power plays such as the following examples.

1. Redefining the Problem

The clue is whether the discussion stays focused on the child and his needs. When parents or their counsel keep moving the discussion onto the topic of the shortcomings of your agency or yourself, a power play may be in operation. If you allow the time to be spent defending yourself or your agency, you have been power-played, successfully.

To neutralize the power play you need to request a return to the subject at hand, namely the child. "I can understand how you might feel that way, but we really need to talk about what you can do to make sure Johnny gets to his doctor's appointments. He can't stay well if he doesn't get his medication. Is transportation a problem?"

Of course, you and the parents and their counsel may see different issues that need attention. A power play is only occurring if you feel the concerns you raise are constantly being diverted to issues that do not have to do with the welfare of the child. Another way to neutralize this power play is to make the diversion overt. "Every time I ask about the doctor's appointments, you start talking about something else. I'm starting to feel frustrated, because this we simply have to deal with this problem. Can we discuss it for a few minutes before we talk about anything else?"

2. Intimidation

Physical intimidation is intended to evoke fear, psychological intimidation is intended to evoke confusion and emotional reaction. Negotiations with opposing counsel before court can lead to a mutually satisfactory resolution, but sometimes intimidation power plays are used. "I hope you don't intend to say that in court." (Or I'll shred you on the witness stand.) "That's not acceptable evidence." (I'm a lawyer, I know what evidence is and you don't.) "All I know is, the family was doing okay until you came along." (*You* are the real problem.) "You're new to the job, right?" (You don't know what you're doing, but I do.) "Well, you'd agree that a bit of supervision would do the trick and everyone would be better off without a long drawn-out court battle." (If you don't go along with my proposal, I'll never let you off the witness stand.)

You can't necessarily tell whether an intimidation power play is being used from the words alone. You need to make a judgment about the motive behind the words. Test the words by stating clearly, without defensiveness, what you agree with and what you don't. If the discussion moves on, fine. If the responses escalate in their apparent provocation, you are being power-played and you may as well terminate the discussion and refer the lawyer to your own counsel.

3. Scarcity: Either-Or

It is fundamental to power plays that they are based on a scarcity mentality. "Either you agree to my proposal or we'll fight it out in court." "If you won't let my client see the child for overnight visits, we'll let the judge decide." The premise presented is that only two choices are available.

Power moves seek acquiescence. One alternative to going along and being controlled is to countermove. "You realize that I'll have to testify about the previous apprehension if you go to court on this one." "Really I wonder whether any visits are appropriate for awhile, just until things cool down." Countermoves keep the competition for control going, by escalating through an assertion of power greater than the first.

The better alternative is to neutralize the power game and identify the common ground in which other options can be considered. The technique involved is the same regardless of what power game is being played. First, decline to make an either-or choice. Second, take enough time to relax and collect your thoughts. Power tactics are intended to disorient and throw you off your track. Third, make your consciousness of the presence of the game overt. "Whether the case goes to court or not is a separate issue. Let me tell you why I don't think overnight visits are a good idea right now." Fourth, address the problem itself, not the way the problem is being presented, and state the facts as you see them, and what you want. "Overnight visits seem too risky to me until the mother and the father have decided whether to stay together. Right now there's too much arguing and fighting, and last week the father got violent. I need to know Johnny will be safe before I'd be prepared to agree to overnight visits. What would your clients be willing to do to prevent a further violent incident?"

By returning the focus to the problem and stating specifically how you see the facts and what you want, you open the discussion to how opposing counsel sees the facts and what she wants. If there is a willingness to proceed cooperatively, you will both be working on the common ground in which, with a little commitment and creativity, the factors may be rearranged to your mutual satisfaction. "Perhaps the grandmother could stay over for a few days. The mom and dad don't fight when she's around." "What about trying a visit for the whole day tomorrow, until suppertime. If that works out a couple of times, maybe we could try an overnight visit."

Almost invariably presentation of the problem in an either-or format results in other options remaining hidden from view. If you encounter strong resistance to putting energy into exploring the options, it is likely that opposing counsel is not serious about negotiating and intends to seek a court contest no matter what.

POWER PLAYS IN COURT

In one sense, power plays are what court is all about. Traditionally, one side seeks to press every advantage and maintain control of the proceeding at the cost of the other side. Protection cases, not being adversarial in the traditional sense, are less subject to legal gamesmanship. Even hotly contested cases concentrate on investigating the facts of the matter. Cross-examination techniques can include power plays, though they occur far less frequently than most social workers believe.

1. Just Answer Yes or No

When you are under cross-examination, counsel is entitled to ask you leading questions and attempt to get you to answer yes or no, without more. Some types of leading questions are classical either-or power plays. "As a professional social worker, you believe a family should stay together, don't you?"

The courtroom is not the place to be overt in identifying the power play, but you can retain your own power by declining to make either-or choices wherever possible. "I can't answer that question with a 'yes' or 'no'." "It depends on the circumstances." Or even, "Some families are far better off when the family members live separately."

This power play is not terribly successful in family court. Family court is not like television or movies, where the questions of courtroom lawyers are written by staffs of entertainment writers. The task in family court is to find out what is really going on in the family. You *are* the caseworker for the family and if you express a need to elaborate beyond a yes or no answer, the judge will usually want to hear what you have to say.

2. Interruptions

In court, interruptions of your responses have the same effect they do outside court. Interruptions are intended to disrupt the thought processes of the speaker and to take over the dominant role in the conversation.

If you are interrupted by counsel who moves on to the next question, you can begin your answer to that one by saying, "I'd like to complete my answer to your last question first."

Repetitive interruptions should evoke objections from your own counsel, who can ask the judge to allow you to complete your answer without interruption. If your counsel permits you to be interrupted without objecting, sit down with him after court and instruct him to object. He may not know whether you want such assistance or not.

3. Rushing

The pressure of cross-examination can be escalated by asking rapid-fire questions without giving a witness time to think about her reply.

You are under no obligation to meet the pace of your questioner. You must answer all the questions asked, but you are entitled to consider your reply.

Take a beat or two before answering. It is difficult for counsel to build up momentum with a careful, thoughtful witness. There is no rush.

4. Fancy Language

Words are the tools of the courtroom lawyer, but it is easy to get carried away. Questions made up of several separate clauses or more than one question may be created by design or excessive enthusiasm for the task at hand.

As a witness you are obliged to answer questions posed, but you are entitled to answer them one at a time. If the question is unclear, ask for clarification. If it was too long for you to be certain about the wording, ask for it to be repeated. If you don't understand what is being asked, tell the judge you don't understand the question.

Counsel who are not power-playing may gracefully concede that they aren't sure themselves what they meant by the question. Counsel who are power-playing may attempt to confuse you with complicated language, but you can neutralize the move easily by saying that you don't understand the question. Never pretend to understand just to avoid admitting you haven't followed what is said. Your answer will probably show that you missed the point anyway, which might make the judge wonder about what else you have missed earlier.

5. Personal Space

There is little dramatic marching back and forth by counsel in an ordinary family court, but occasionally counsel may approach you physically for some reason.

If you feel uncomfortable by the proximity, express it. "Excuse me, would you mind stepping back a bit? I feel uncomfortable when you stand so close to me."

6. Water Torture

Counsel may seem to ask you the same question several times. You may answer it the same way each time. It remains a mystery as to why this happens so often. Perhaps it is hoped that you will forget the answer you just gave, or that eventually you will get tired and make a mistake.

Possibly counsel is just trying to irritate you a little, to see if you will express your irritation. Or perhaps counsel can't remember the next question and is treading water.

Be patient as the judge, who generally will be "reluctant to interfere with counsel's conduct of the case." Resign yourself. If counsel has all day, so have you.

7. Eye Contact

It is a cliche that you can see the soul itself by looking into someone's eyes. Some counsel believe they have *your* soul in the palm of their hands, so long as you maintain eye contact with them.

What counsel are counting on is your natural tendency, as a member of the helping professions, to look at the person you are communicating with. Some social workers have never practiced carrying on a conversation with someone without looking at that person. They are easy prey. So long as you maintain eye contact you are subject to any other body language messages that counsel wants to pass along the conduit.

Notice how police officers testify with their eyes directed to the judge throughout. Indeed, it is the judge to whom your answers are addressed ultimately, even if someone else is asking you the questions. If opposing counsel seems to lock eyes with you, spend the rest of your time on the stand facing the judge.

This is not a matter of always facing the judge in every case. It is a question of whether *you* control your eye-contact habits, or allow them to be controlled by others. If watching opposing counsel makes you feel powerless, reclaim your power by looking elsewhere, and by practicing the curious ability of replying to questions asked by one person through directing your answer to someone else.

8. Not Swallowing the Bait

In all of the examples above of alternative answers to power plays in court, it is vital that you maintain a neutrality of tone. That is, the statement "I really don't understand the question" can carry with it the meaning of the words alone, or it may be laced with hints of sarcasm, boredom, irritability, anger, haughtiness, or apology.

None of these is appropriate. In fact, using emotional tone to contradict and transcend the literal meaning of the words used is a countermove that escalates the power play. Opposing counsel who can provoke emotional reactions through tone of voice will be quietly delighted, for two reasons.

First, she is more experienced in passing barbs in court than you are and will likely win any contest you choose to enter. Second, she knows the judge will not be impressed by any professional witness who is emotionally self-indulgent on the stand. If opposing counsel handles things right and you continue to react, she may be able to present the court with a solid foundation for wondering just how calm and collected you are capable of being outside of court, particularly when you are working with the family.

Speak simply, clearly, calmly. Leave making points to counsel who are so inclined.

COURT HABITS FOR EVERY CASE

The number one court habit for every case is preparation. You can't invent your case on the witness stand. No factor so affects the persuasiveness and credibility of your presentation of your case as does thorough preparation.

The preparation factor and the court habits associated with collecting the evidence are dealt with in detail in Chapter 8.

The following is a list of practical court habits to take with you every time you appear on the witness stand. The more comfortable and confident you are about applying these in *all* your cases, as a matter of professional habit, the more effective you will be in every individual case.

1. Be Neutral, Fair, Even-Handed

You are not in court to "win." You are in court to present *all* the evidence you have, including evidence which supports the child being returned home.

Any presentation of your evidence which hints that you are telling less than the full story amounts to an escalation of the adversarial quality of the proceeding, requiring opposing counsel to dig for the full picture and hunt for suggestions of unfairness. Patent neutrality and fairness removes the target.

2. Be Clear About Your Mandate, Your Role in Court, the Judge's Role, the Role of Opposing Counsel

Each player in the court process has a role to play. It will be immediately apparent from the manner in which you conduct yourself on the witness stand whether you are clear about the roles involved or not.

It is reasonable for the other players to expect you to be able to express your mandate, both in terms of its central principles and its limitations.

Test yourself by explaining these points out loud to a friend or colleague. If there are fuzzy edges, review Chapter 1 to see if myths or stereotypes are getting in the way.

3. Give Credit to the Parent Early in Your Testimony

Allegations of personal bias against the parents are not uncommon. Put yourself in opposing counsel's shoes. If you heard a social worker speak no good at all about your clients, wouldn't *you* wonder whether bias might be involved?

Pre-empt this red herring by being clear in your mind before you take the stand about the specific, positive things you can say about the parents. Then say them on the stand, within the first few minutes of your testimony.

So long as your testimony includes no positive points, opposing counsel is obliged to monitor this issue and consider raising it in cross-examination. Giving credit to the parents early on puts this issue to rest in advance.

4. Concede Error Readily

You are not expected to be perfect. Where mistakes have been made, both opposing counsel and the judge will be watching to see how you handle yourself.

Apparent resistance to conceding error can be more damaging to your credibility than the mistake itself.

Watch seasoned expert witnesses. They are accustomed to conceding error readily, doing so in a relaxed manner that enhances their credibility rather than diminishing it.

5. If You Don't Know the Answer, Say So

You are not expected to know everything. Observe good expert witnesses on this point. The best demonstrate great clarity about what they know and what they don't know. Being seen as comfortable about admitting what you don't know enhances your credibility when you later express certainty about other facts. Appearing reluctant to admit that which you don't know calls the rest of your evidence into question.

6. Avoid Jargon

Describe what you heard and saw. Use of professional jargon has two negative side effects. It irritates some judges considerably, since social worker jargon is not information which the legal system is designed to ingest. You are expected to know that. It also subtly diminishes the role of the judge. It is for the judge to determine, for example, if certain behavior is "inappropriate." If *you* describe the behavior as "inappropriate," you are taking the role of the judge and leaving the judge without the facts he needs to make his own assessment.

Give the court the facts and allow the court to draw the conclusions from them. Jargon tends to mask the facts, as well as move the focus of your testimony from the child and his situation to yourself as witness.

7. Maintain Eye Contact with the Judge

Ultimately the judge is the one you are on the witness stand to communicate with, regardless of whether questions come from your counsel or opposing counsel. If you maintain eye contact solely with your questioners, you lose important information about how the judge is taking your testimony.

Judges make notes. You can't pace your testimony properly if you don't keep an eye on the judicial pen. If it is drawing ships and boats, move on. There may also be a tiny irritation factor involved. What do *you* feel like when the person addressing you refuses to look at you?

8. Decline Eye Contact with Opposing Counsel

This is not an absolute rule. If you are skilled and comfortable with controlling your eye contact, do as you see fit.

The point is that when cross-examination is aggressive, it is easier to maintain your focus on the content of the questions rather than the manner in which they are asked if you keep your eyes on the judge.

9. Keep the Focus on the Child

Under the pressure of cross-examination many questions may seem to you to be about side issues that have little to do with the case at hand. As a witness you are obliged to answer the question asked, but often you can use your answer to bring the focus back to the child and his family situation. That is, after all, the ultimate reason you are on the witness stand in the first place.

10. Don't Argue

As a witness you are not in court to object to the nature or quality of questions you are asked. This is your counsel's task. You are there to answer the questions.

A "prickly" witness is a delight to opposing counsel. A witness who engages in argument with opposing counsel commits several errors of professional judgment. Credibility with the court is diminished, as the judge must wonder why a professional witness misunderstands the task at hand.

Some questions are deliberately provocative. The judge is interested to know whether you are easily provoked. He is usually not particularly interested in the content of your answer to such a maneuver, any more than opposing counsel is. Demonstrate your awareness of what is really going on by declining to rise to the bait. Just answer the question, calmly and simply.

These are a sample of practical witness skills. Assess your own skill level on these points. Monitor how you are doing in cases as you go along. The goal is to make them second nature to you, to make them regular court habits that you bring to bear on every case. Make the goal a conscious part of your professional agenda. Role-playing outside of court is very helpful for practicing the ones you have trouble with.

TRANSFORMING THE SOCIAL WORKER TOOLBAG

By this point you should be noticing that skills required for effective court performance are mainly just variations of communications skills you already use all the time.

Feeling powerless and intimidated about court process is just a choice. The choice is premised on seeing the courtroom as a radically different environment. If it is seen that way, it will be experienced that way.

Choosing to see the courtroom as just another part of your working territory enables you to bring your full toolbag of skills along with you.

Choosing to notice how the same skills you use in the field apply in court provides a solid foundation for confidence when you take the stand.

Committing yourself to development of a repertoire of practical court habits which you apply to every case eliminates the need to invent the wheel when you are on the witness stand.

Court process is not mysterious or unfathomable. The clues to being effective there need not be sought from some magical external source. Your toolbag is *already* full. You need only transform the toolbag to meet the modified needs of court process. This requires a degree of energy and commitment, but it need not be a struggle.

POWER PARITY

It is in the nature of the adversarial system that players in the process are inclined to attempt to establish control over others. The result is that some players use power games so frequently that they become a matter of habit as much as anything else.

Power moves presented in the court process are perhaps more subtle or more intense versions of ones you encounter in the field. It is a waste of energy to spend time wishing that they won't occur from time to time.

Develop your own judgment about when power moves are occurring. The key to neutralizing power moves is to decline to play. Countermoves merely escalate the competitive forces involved. You need to respond to a power move with power parity; that is, with sufficient power to neutralize the move, but not so much that the situation is escalated.

Becoming skilled in applying power parity permits power games to be transcended. The goal is to discover the common ground on which both parties can state the facts as they see them and the results they each want, such that additional choices can be discovered which are mutually satisfactory.

You have as much power as anyone else. Watch the way you handle invitations to give it away. You can't prevent such invitations from being made, but you can decline to accept them, if you choose.

"DO YOU HAVE CHILDREN OF YOUR OWN?"

This particular cross-examination question provokes such common irritation that it warrants a little section of its own. The question, in fact, rarely arises, but at some point or other it will occur. So let's put it into perspective.

The objection to it is along the lines of, "Why should counsel be entitled to ask personal questions?" or "What does whether or not I have children have to do with this protection case?"

The context of the question is the widely accepted folk belief that you can't know anything about parenting if you don't have children. This slippery little notion purports to give a justification for asking the question. Social workers are often tempted to challenge the question and ask who will prevent it from being asked.

No one will.

Fair or not, most judges will be reluctant to prevent opposing counsel from asking, in effect, what personal experience a worker has with children. After all, you have removed a child from his family on the basis of concerns about the child. It is not particularly unreasonable, in light of this action, to inquire about the kind of personal experience you have which informs your judgment.

This is not to say that the judge will give much weight to your answer one way or the other. The point is that the question is considered fair game, in the main, so it is wasted energy to deal with it by fruitless objection.

The better tactic is to accept that the issue will come up in one case or another eventually, and to anticipate and prepare for it. Give some thought to what your practice will be in dealing with personal questions.

One childless social worker, for example, when asked whether she has any children herself, makes it a practice to pause and reply, "Yes, I think I have 24 cases at the moment." Your own reply need not be so elegant, but you would do well to consider how you would respond to this question. Keep a pleasant reply or two in stock.

Most people can list quite extensive experience with children if they put their minds to it. Consider spending an hour or so to make a complete list of every personal experience you have had with children and their care. "I have a statement of my experience with children if you would like to see it" can be a very effective reply. It communicates that you have anticipated the question and prepared to deal with it fully.

Some social workers prefer to give calm, brief replies, with a tolerant, slightly curious expression that the question should be asked at all.

The judge will be more interested in how you handle the question than what the content of your answer is.

The place to find out what type of reply works for you is *not* in the courtroom. It is beforehand, at home or at work, perhaps roleplaying the issue on the premise that the question will be asked at some point or another.

Most litigation is about money or property, not family matters, so most witnesses are not subject to questions about their family lives. Protection cases are all about families, so questions about your own personal experiences are, on their face, admissible.

The judge knows, as does opposing counsel, that facts about your personal marital status have little to do with the case. You are a professional, with professional qualifications and experience, which is what you base your decisions on. Assessment of your professional expertise does not rest on your personal life.

You can instruct your counsel to attempt to object to personal questions if you wish. The preferable approach is to answer such questions calmly and briefly, without appearing defensive or irritated. Handling the matter this way enhances your professionalism. If you choose not to be provoked, opposing counsel will quickly drop this line of questioning and move on. If producing replies is like pulling teeth, she may prefer to spend some time on the subject, the better to attempt to reveal you as "touchy" and "over-sensitive."

It may help you to bear in mind the reason you are in court. You are there for the child. Remaining focused on this fact does much to reduce the tribulations of court process to nonevents.

Chapter 5

PROTECTION STATUTES: AN OVERVIEW

THE STATE AS A SILVER CLOUD

Visualize the powers embodied in your protection statute as a silver cloud, suspended over the entire jurisdiction. Below, some kids live with both parents, others with only one or perhaps a relative. The legal rights of the adults, whether they be guardianship, custody, or access, have been settled by court order or separation, or are a matter of law. These rights prevail unless the child is at risk. When you intervene to remove a child, it is as if the silver cloud descends, temporarily overriding all other individual rights in the interest of protecting the child.

In the course of a period of state wardship the rights of the individual citizens involved may alter. Custody rights may change between one adult and another through a family court application or through changes to a separation agreement.

Strictly speaking, such changes in custody rights between individual citizens have nothing to do with you. As the representative of the state, of society as a whole, you are *not* mandated to seek improved custody arrangements for children, unless specifically ordered to investigate private custody matters by a court.

Upon the termination of a wardship order, the silver cloud lifts and rights relating to the child are once more a matter of law between private citizens. The practical result is that the child must be returned to his custodial parent, but who this is may have changed through legal action in the intervening period.

Due to the wide-ranging nature of services offered to families, some social workers maintain a fuzzy view of how far their powers extend. There are two important limitations on the powers of a social worker.

First, although the legal language in protection statutes varies from one jurisdiction to another, the principle at stake is the same everywhere: intervention by the state in private family matters is justified only when the child is at risk and requires protection not being provided by the parents. This is the mandate under which you and the silver cloud operate. No jurisdiction empowers social workers to interfere in private custodial arrangements just because the social worker feels changes in custody or access would be in the best interests of the child. The state is not mandated to impose custody arrangements on families; this remains a private matter for individual citizens to resolve as they will.

Second, every protection statute includes provision for the child to be reunited with his parent or parents if at all possible. The discretion as to which parent the child should be returned to is limited by the private custodial arrangements in place at the time return is contemplated. Choosing to return the child to the noncustodial parent, in the face of an agreement or court order granting custody rights to the other parent, is generally not a choice available to a social worker.

From the perspective of the protection mandate, you are entitled to take the view that a child would not be safe if returned to the parent who has formal custody, and to make further protection applications accordingly. If you express views as to which parent would be the better custodial parent, you are overstepping the protection mandate and may find yourself drawn into a private custody dispute as a witness. Counsel in that proceeding may legitimately inquire into the basis of the authority you are claiming to intervene in private citizens' custody matters, unless you have been ordered by a court to prepare a custody report.

This distinction between the grounds for state intervention in private family affairs, and legal disputes between private citizens concerning their children, is one which every protection social worker must be clear about.

Occasionally legal proceedings under the protection statute may occur just before, or just after, or at the same time as parties engage in a separate dispute concerning custody or access. Sometimes these two separate proceedings—state vs. family, and citizen vs. citizen—may be "joined" so that evidence on both cases will be heard by the same court at the same time.

Notice the distinction in the two legal issues to be decided by the court. In the protection case the issue is whether the quality of care of the child has fallen below minimal standards (as defined in the local protection statute) such that state intervention is found to be warranted. In the custody case the issue is whether it would be in the best interests of the child to be in the custody of one parent rather than another.

If the court directs that a protection case be joined with a custody dispute, you may be asked, through your counsel, to take a position as to which case should be heard first.

When this occurs you need to consider your view of each parent in terms of your protection mandate. If you consider that neither parent, regardless of any change in legal custody, can adequately protect the child, you may request that the protection case be heard first. Where you have investigated the parent who now seeks custody and have no protection concerns about him or her, you may suggest that the custody dispute proceed first, as it may result in no further need to pursue the protection proceeding at all.

Find out from your counsel about local practice when a private citizen custody dispute and a protection case occur at the same time.

JUDICIAL AND SOCIAL AMBIVALENCE

Courts and legislatures have wrestled over the proper way to deal with neglected or abused children for a long time. No one wants government, through your agency, to have an unfettered right to intervene in private family life. This concern has resulted in a variety of statutory attempts to nail down with ever-increasing specificity those circumstances which justify your intervention in the first place.

None of these attempts has been overwhelmingly successful. The reality in the field is that the circumstances of family life are so varied, involving so many constellations of factors affecting risk to the child, that intervention is still largely a matter of social worker discretion.

The result of the lack of practical statutory guidance is that it is difficult to predict how a court is likely to respond to the facts of a particular case. In earlier times, when faith in the powers of social workers to effect human change were much higher, courts would virtually rubber stamp most of the agency's applications. Today faith in the ability of government to change individuals is more limited. This is also reflected in a diminishing of resources available to social workers to offer concrete help to families, which in turn has resulted in the courts being less inclined to accept that a child is necessarily better off in agency care.

On the other hand, the statistics about child neglect and abuse are frightening. The creation of mechanisms to facilitate reporting, along with a broader social understanding of the extent of child neglect and abuse, has resulted in enormous increases of the reports received by social agencies. According to the American Humane Association, there were 2,178,000 such reports in 1987, compared to 512,000 in 1977 and 13,133 in 1970. In Canada the federal Committee on Sexual Offences Against Children and Youths reported in 1984 (the Badgley Report) that one in four girls was likely to have been sexually abused by the time she reached the age of eighteen.

It is an extreme understatement to remark that social service resources have not escalated in parallel to reports of the extent of the problem.

Greater public interest in child protection issues has produced some ambivalent results. Far more attention is given to the task of accumulating and investigating reports of abuse and neglect than on providing adequate service to cases once the reports are verified. Physical abuse, especially sexual abuse, always commands greater public interest than the far more widespread problem of child neglect. More and more social workers are exposed to professional negligence actions by parents (see *The Vulnerable Social Worker,* by Douglas Besharov), or held accountable by private action groups created to challenge the propriety of state intervention.

In short, the days are gone when the protection social worker's word was automatically accepted at face value. The court and the legal system hold social workers accountable for intervention decisions, and require that protection cases be proven with legal evidence that meets a high standard. A social worker's ability to collect legal evidence and present it effectively in court is now a critical factor determining whether, in fact, a child can be protected.

INTERIM CUSTODY

Most protection statutes provide for a summary interim custody hearing of some sort shortly after the intervention, with a full hearing on the case later on. The period between the two hearings is to be used by the social worker to fully investigate the case, with the results of the investigation to be presented at the full hearing.

Become familiar with local practice under your own statute. Often the expectations of the court at the first hearing are significantly lower than at the full hearing later on. Some statutes provide that the purpose of the first hearing is primarily to determine where the child should live, pending the completion of the investigation and the full hearing.

There is an increasing trend on the part of parents and their counsel, and some judges, to attempt to deal with the case as a whole on the first appearance in court. The desirability of prompt response by the legal system to a family intervention is not questionable. However, the time between the initial intervention and the full airing of the evidence has to be sufficient to enable you to complete a proper intervention.

Obtain specific advice from your counsel as to the expectations of the court on your first appearance. Local practice may require far more of you than first appears from a reading of your protection statute.

SERVING NOTICES

Protection statutes require that parents be served with some form of notice of the agency's application at the full hearing. Often it is the social worker's responsibility to serve the notices on the parties, or to arrange for their service.

It is understandable for this task to come to be regarded as "just paperwork," draining time away from more important concerns. However, this attitude reflects a serious misconception of the purpose of serving notice.

The two objectives of giving formal notice are to let adults significant in the life of the child (at a minimum, both parents) know that a problem has occurred of sufficient importance to warrant intervention, and to protect the jurisdiction of the court. It is fundamental to legal proceedings that, except in extraordinary circumstances, parties who are to be subject to a decision of the court are entitled to know about the application ahead of time. A failure to serve a party is not merely a mistake in the paperwork; the court may be obliged to dismiss the application without considering its merits, if notice on someone was not served.

Sometimes social workers accede to the request of the custodial parent, whom they know well, not to serve notice on the other parent for fear of subsequent action on the custody issue. This is also a misconception of what a protection proceeding involves. It is, in effect, the right of the child to have significant adults in his life informed of legal action, in order that they may offer themselves as a resource if they wish. It is not for the social worker to prejudge the appropriate involvement of the other parent by not letting him or her know of the application. Such a failure to serve may be fatal to the court's jurisdiction to proceed with the hearing.

Protection statutes vary in how they define the parties required to be served with notice, and in how they define who a "parent" is. You do not want to place the child in the position of being ordered returned to a parent for failure to serve the required parties. If you are uncertain about whether a certain party needs to be served (for example, an aunt who has cared for the child for several months), get advice from your counsel or ask for a ruling from the court. If you do not find out until the hearing date that someone should have been served, it may then be too late and the court may be obliged to dismiss your application without hearing evidence.

The formalities of serving notice are critical to maintaining the power of the court to hear your application. If your protection statute states that the parties *shall* be served with notice before a hearing commences, the court will be statute-bound from hearing substantive evidence unless this is done.

Defects in serving notice can result in the child being returned to the situation of risk from which you removed him. The ability to correctly serve notices is consequently fundamental to your ability to effectively provide protection to a child.

THE TWO-STEP PROTECTION HEARING

Whether the full hearing of the protection case takes only a few minutes, as in an application which is unopposed or by consent, or several days of trial, as in a hotly contested case, the hearing itself nevertheless involves two distinct stages.

The first is the "adjudicative" portion, referred to hereafter as the "finding" step. This is the part of the hearing in which the evidence about the application is presented to enable the court to make a "finding" as to whether or not the child is in need of protection.

If the court decides that the evidence does not support a finding that the child is in need of protection, the child will be ordered returned home.

If the court finds the child in need of protection, the hearing moves on to the "dispositional" step. This is the part of the case that has to do with the evidence about what kind of protection order is in the best interests of the child.

Protection statutes which break up this process into two separate hearings make the role of the social worker in court much easier. As with a criminal proceeding, evidence at the first stage has largely to do with past events; if an accused is found guilty, the evidence at the separate sentencing stage is much more future-oriented and predictive. Protection hearings similarly look first at what has happened in the past and then move on to consider what arrangement is best for the future.

Confusion arises under statutes in which all the evidence is heard in a single hearing.

The best way of illustrating the confusion is to consider the status of the social worker as an expert or nonexpert witness. Nonexpert witnesses (ordinary witnesses) can only testify about their personal observations. Expert witnesses can express opinions about events, once they are "qualified" as experts. To be qualified as an expert means that the credentials of the expert are presented to the court, along with identification of the area of expertise claimed on behalf of the expert. Upon acceptance of the qualifications of the expert, she is entitled to express opinions in court.

Opinion evidence may be given great weight by the judge, or little or none at all. Proof of a fact, as opposed to an opinion, must be accepted by the judge unless contradictory proof is presented.

Whether social workers qualify as expert witnesses depends upon the particular social worker as well as local practice. Social workers are qualified as experts in the same way as other expert witnesses, which is described in Chapter 6. But some courts are more reluctant than others to allow social workers to express opinion, other than concerning planning issues. Proof that a particular social worker has special expertise and experience is sufficient to qualify a social worker as an expert in most courts.

Even when a social worker is not qualified as an expert witness, the expertise issue can create confusion when testifying under a protection statute providing only for a single hearing of the "finding" evidence along with the "dispositional" evidence.

In such a single hearing there is no distinct signal to inform the social worker of the point at which the hearing has moved from one stage to the other. Confusion arises when the social worker finds herself subject to objections from opposing counsel whenever she attempts to express an opinion about the case, only to find herself later on *invited* to express opinions, even by opposing counsel.

The answer lies in the distinction between the different issues to be dealt with at each of the two stages. The social worker's evidence in support of the finding needs to be based on personal observations and facts. If you describe a father as "drunk" when you arrived for a home visit, your testimony will be objected to as opinion evidence. That is, are you claiming special expertise in being able to assess whether or not an individual is drunk? Do you have special training or qualifications that support such expertise?

It is far better in any event to confine yourself to the facts during the finding stage of the proceeding. The expertise issue aside, expressing opinions tends to remove vital factual evidence from consideration by the judge. Describe your observations—the father had bloodshot eyes, he was unsteady on his feet, his speech was slurred—and let the *court* draw the *conclusion* from the facts. When you offer up the conclusions directly, you provoke an inquiry into whether you are qualified to draw such conclusions, as well as depriving the court of the opportunity to do its job as the "finder of facts."

During the finding phase of the hearing you should avoid opinion evidence and relate the facts and observations instead. The dispositional stage is quite different, because here the court is no longer concerned with what happened in the past but what is the best arrangement for the future. In effect the evidence to be heard is predictive, and who better to offer predictions about what plan will work best than yourself? Your "expertise" in expressing opinions about the plan is rarely placed in question.

Notice the unique element involved in this aspect of protection proceedings. In other litigation apart from family matters, the case goes to court, a judgment is rendered, and that's the end of it. In a protection case the court must make the order the judge considers will have the best chance to deal with the problems over the next period of time, and the case may well return to court for review and further orders. Courts are more usually expected to rule on what has happened in the past, not to design the future.

If you have been confused by how your opinions sometimes provoke objection and sometimes are deliberately sought, you may not be making a clear enough distinction between the two stages of the hearing, especially if your statute requires all the evidence to be heard at one time. Notice what issue is being dealt with at the time of an objection that you are expressing an opinion. Odds are good that such objections are occurring when you are testifying about what has happened to justify a finding that the child was in need of protection. Stick to the facts when you are describing the past. When you are testifying about what kind of order would be in the best interests of the child, you are talking about the future. At this stage it is quite proper for you, given your experience with the family, to give the court your opinion about whether a particular access arrangement would likely work, how often visits should take place, or what length of order is required to allow enough time for family problems to be dealt with. The court must determine disposition for itself, but your assessment of what is likely to work and what is not is important information for the court to hear.

THE MANDATE TO RETURN THE CHILD

Whatever the wording of your particular protection statute, the mandate to protect children is balanced by an equally powerful mandate to return children home wherever possible. State intervention is not justified on the basis that a child would be "better off" living in a foster home. It is not a question of the "best interests" of the child. Intervention is justified only when the child is "at risk" to an extent that the state must become involved.

When conditions have changed during the term of an order such that it is safe for the child to be returned home, the mandate is to do so, as soon as possible. Again, it is not a question of whether the child would be "better off" if he continued to live in care. The issue is only whether the risk which precipitated the intervention has been sufficiently mitigated that the child will be provided with minimally acceptable standards of care at home.

As a protection social worker you must maintain a clear conceptualization of the limitations on your mandate. Personally, you may well consider, as do many of the other players in court, that a child would be more likely to flourish if he were not returned home. But no one has a mandate to run around attempting to improve the lives of children in general. The bottom line is that the state is *not responsible* for the lives of children and families unless and until, and only for so long as, the family standard of care falls below a point that puts a child at risk.

The legal system is a clumsy instrument for facilitating the gentle return home of a child. Most often, the parents are simply entitled to the return of the child upon termination of the protection order, period. This change in environments is jarring for any child.

To take account of this your planning should include a gradual "phasing in" of the return whenever possible. As the expiry date of the protection order approaches, frequency and length of access visits should be increased, to include overnight visits eventually. The legal system does not have the capacity to fine-tune a gradual transition, but you do. How you intend to go about it, and under what conditions, are points you need to address during the original hearing.

VISITATION AND EXPECTATIONS

The whole subject of visitation arrangements and expectations of the parents also reveals the uniqueness of protection proceedings as compared to most litigation the legal system deals with. Tinkering with plans for the immediate future, making adjustments as you go along, and constantly monitoring and reviewing the situation are just not required following most court orders, but these elements are critical in a protection proceeding.

Where problems are such that concrete, specific steps taken by the parents will improve the likelihood that the problems will be resolved, the expectations of the parents should be made crystal clear, preferably on paper. It is important that the expectations be achievable, and that events can be monitored closely enough so there is concrete information about how well things are going. This will be important evidence at a further application hearing, if one is required.

By filing a written statement of expectations at the time of the protection hearing, you will ensure that misunderstandings about who was to do what will be avoided. The statement should be specific about what services you agree to provide and what steps the parents agree to take. Should a further application be necessary, the statement will make it much easier for the court to determine how well both sides have lived up to the agreed upon expectations.

Protection statutes normally enable a court to fine-tune terms of access, but this is not always desirable. Under the umbrella of a court order providing for "reasonable access," any number of different schemes of visitation are possible. If the time and date of each access visit is sought to be spelled out in the court order, an application to vary the order will be necessary if circumstances change, as they often do.

If visitation arrangements are not spelled out in detail in the court order, they certainly should be between yourself and the parent. Put the scheme in writing if you anticipate any misunderstandings at all. The facts surrounding how access visits have been handled both by yourself and by the parents are of critical importance to the court in a later decision about whether it is safe for the child to return home. A detailed record of access visits is also important for the additional information visits provide about the relationship between the child and his parents. It is not unusual for this additional information to turn out to be more important in determining how the case evolves than information about the incident which triggered your original involvement with the family.

The legal system does not have the time to handle frequent review of access problems, but you should not hesitate to return to court if there are serious disagreements about what kind of access should be happening.

Your protection statute is the legal framework defining the limits of your mandate to protect children. To work effectively within this framework, you need to develop a clear conceptualization of the competing values which the statute attempts to balance. A working familiarity with the principles at stake ensures that your protection statute is a source of strength in your court work. Otherwise, the formal statutory requirements can become dangerous obstacles to protecting children from risk.

Chapter 6

TRUTH:
THE MISTRESS OF MANY FACES

THE SEPARATE REALITY OF COURT

An old joke talks about six blind men standing around an elephant, each describing what he thinks the animal is on the basis of information about the appendage he is standing beside. The joke is used in law schools to demonstrate how unreliable the testimony of witnesses can be in getting at the "truth."

It is axiomatic that viewpoint determines the view. What is observed to be happening has much to do with the premises, biases, and belief systems of the observer. Events are seen differently depending on whether they are viewed from psychological, philosophical, political, or sociological perspectives. The "raw facts" may be the same, but as human beings we tend to allow into awareness those facts that conform to our internal maps of reality, and disregard the rest.

The legal system goes about determining the truth in a manner quite different from approaches used by members of the helping professions. Confusion can arise if you attempt to import the belief systems of the social work profession into the forum of the courtroom. It is not necessary for you to choose between the different approaches to determine the truth. It is necessary to notice what the approach of the legal system is, so that you can deal with it on its own terms.

The separate reality of court process determines the truth with the full force of its own authority behind it. In an important way, what the court decides to be true *is* the truth in practical terms.

For example, you may be convinced that many of the family's problems are related to the fact that the father is alcoholic. He denies the alcoholism, which you regard as a confirmation of it. You have no direct evidence of the amount or frequency of the father's drinking, but the patterns in the family relationships are familiar to you as characteristic of alcoholic families.

In court you testify about the patterns you observe. Opposing counsel challenges the circularity of your approach. That is, she points out that if the father admitted his drinking problem, you would regard the admission as evidence of the problem. If he denies it, you regard the denial as evidence of the problem. No matter what he says, you are determined to conclude he abuses alcohol. She points out to the judge that no provable *facts* have been presented in evidence one way or another. The only fact presented about the issue at all is the fact that the father denies a drinking problem.

On this evidence the judge makes a finding of fact that there is no evidence to prove the father abuses alcohol. You feel betrayed by the legal system. The alcoholism issue is central to your neglect case. What more could you have done?

Well, a great deal. The court is a separate reality with known rules about the type and quality of information acceptable to it. It is vested by society with the power and authority to determine the truth, but it can only do so on the basis of the information presented to it. Declining to observe the rules fundamental to court process is not merely naive; it can result in the child being returned to the situation of risk from which you removed him.

Being effective in court requires that you make a conscious decision to honor the separate reality of court process. How you come to terms with this reality is up to you; *whether* you accept it or not is not an issue, since you must. When the court decides that a child is not in need of protection, that is the end of it. Unless the judge has made a legal error justifying an appeal, you are just as obliged to accept the court's findings of facts as the parent is when the child is found to require state care.

For practical purposes, if the court decides, for example, that the child will be safe if overnight visits are allowed, you are *obliged* to demonstrate respect for the law's authority by proceeding on the premise that he will be safe. A failure to present sufficiently persuasive evidence in the first place cannot be remedied by substituting your own views for those of the court. This reaction is what contempt of court is all about.

Notice how much energy you invest in resistance to the legal system's approach to establishing "truth." Notice whether you "prove" the invalidity of the legal system's approach by declining to present the type of evidence it can accept, "proving" the flaws of the system by creating results which are the opposite of the ones you want. Whether your criticisms are valid or not is beside the point. The net result is that the child is not protected. This is, after all, the only reason you go to court in the first place.

INTUITION ON THE WITNESS STAND

Intuition is the power of knowing something without being able to point to identifiable information. The truth that you know through your powers of intuition is not less valid in any ultimate sense than the truths you can present through provable facts. In fact, since social workers tend to have highly developed powers of intuition, what you know intuitively often has more to do with the truth of what is really going on than the observable facts would suggest—that is what intuition is all about.

Courts of law do not make decisions based on intuition, although judges and lawyers can be very intuitive about witnesses. It is a serious mistake for a professional witness to start off her testimony by relating her intuitions. Objections will be based on describing such evidence as mere opinion, or irrelevant, or inadmissible, but objections will surely be made. Your primary purpose on the witness stand is to tell the court about the observations you have made. Just the facts, ma'am.

Still, there are two aspects to the process where you can apply your intuitive talents. One is by way of monitoring the judge and opposing counsel. You can pick up significant information about how these players in the process view the case and what their real concerns are, beyond what is said formally. The neutral stone-face is an available persona in the repertoire of any courtroom player, but intuition transcends surfaces. By discussing what you pick up in this manner with your counsel or with colleagues later, your grip on the case will continue to improve.

The other point at which your intuition comes into play is when you are invited to express it, in the future-oriented second stage of a protection case. The judge or other players may ask you directly whether you think an access arrangement will work, or whether a problem will be solved in three months rather than six. The questions may be framed in terminology more acceptable to the legal system ("As a seasoned social worker who has worked with the family for a long time, what do you think of . . . "), but it is the use of your intuition that is being sought.

In addition, your intuitions are useful in preparing the case for court. How will this witness come across? How will the court react to this piece of evidence? What tone and language will work best to describe this event in the case? Presenting a case in court is not mere mechanics and the court is not a machine. The legal system is fundamentally a human system. Intuition can reveal a great deal about who the human beings are and what they want.

RUMOR, GOSSIP, AND SCURRILOUS INNUENDO

In the field you obtain an enormous quantity of information from a wide variety of sources. Sometimes you assess the reliability of the information almost automatically, deciding which alleged facts need to be investigated further for verification.

The legal system proceeds on the basis that the only facts which count are those which have been verified. In the field you make your own judgments as you go along as to which of the rumor, gossip, and scurrilous innuendo coming your way is worth pondering further. In court none of this secondhand information is acceptable as evidence. The formal term is "hearsay," statements made by parties who are not present in court and who are therefore unavailable for cross-examination to test the reliability of their statements.

To be effective in using the courts to help you protect kids, you need to keep a constant eye on later court process as you acquire secondhand information. What is properly acceptable as a basis for a social work decision is not necessarily acceptable for a legal decision. To be of use in court, you need to speak to sources of secondhand information directly. If your assessment is that the information is relevant and reliable, consider instructing your counsel to call the source as a witness.

You will not likely be permitted to quote secondhand information on the witness stand yourself. You are there to relate your personal observations only, not the alleged observations of others. If you are permitted to quote secondhand information, the odds are good that the judge is nevertheless disregarding it in forming his decision, or is giving it very little weight since opposing counsel has had no opportunity to test the statements through cross-examination.

It is fundamental to legal process that cases must be proven and decisions cannot be made on the basis of statements by witnesses who are not present.

SELF—FULFILLING PROPHESIES

It is common for social workers to have a case conference about a disturbed, abused, or neglected child, with a view to seeing whether there is adequate evidence for court.

It is axiomatic, for example, to assume that a young child who is sexually aggressive has been abused, and to review the case to see what facts suggest how the abuse came about and who perpetrated it. If a child has not been receiving required medical attention, the file is reviewed to see if there is evidence that the parents are inattentive to meeting their own medical needs as well. If a mother is seen as being addicted to abuse to the point that she repeatedly kicks out her violent mate only to take him back again, a claim that she is "separated for good" will be examined for facts demonstrating her true ambivalency.

An estimation of the strength of the case can certainly be determined by these standard methods. There is a demonstrable shortfall, though, which is illustrated by observing the legal system's opposite approach to establishing the "facts" of the case.

The starting point for the legal system is the facts themselves. Piled one upon the other in court, the proven facts form the basis of the conclusions ultimately drawn by the judge.

In contrast, a social worker case conference tends to start from the working premise about the family members, and then to move immediately to ferret out the facts that support the premise, and particularly to consider whether the specific facts would be acceptable proof in a court of law.

The frequent gap in the case conference approach is that the premise is not challenged. Often the working premise is not even discussed in any detail; it is *assumed* to be in operation, such that the sole task is to identify facts which prove its presence. Generally, if some facts are considered not to be acceptable proof in court, the conference members move on to consider other facts, without ever considering the validity of the premise itself.

The result is that sometimes the first time serious consideration is given to the validity of the premise is when opposing counsel challenges it in court.

A preferable approach in terms of preparing for court is to use *some* portion of conference time to consciously challenge the working premise. *Is* the mother ambivalent about the violent relationship? What evidence is there to support the alternative premise; namely, that she's finally finished with the guy? *Do* the parents defer meeting their own medical needs? If so, what are reasonable explanations for doing so, *other than* neglect of themselves as an extrapolation of neglect for their child? Indeed, *were* the child's needs for medical attention truly unmet? Are there alternative explanations for why this took place *other than* the wilful neglect of the parents? *Is* the child sexually aggressive? What *are* the types of sexual behavior within the range of "normal" for a child of this age? What are the *specific* acts of this child which are unusual, and are there *any* alternative explanations about how these acts might have occurred, other than as a result of sexual abuse?

Without use of *some* time to challenge the assumptions which are readily accepted by everyone at the conference, you will be caught by surprise at the challenges asserted in court. You also leave yourself open to opposing counsel's portrayal of your case as a self-fulfilling prophesy, in that, having assumed that an issue was present, your case consists of nothing more than hunting around for evidence to verify your own assumption.

In court skills training workshops for social workers, an entirely new level of understanding of a scenario occurs if you invite participants to consider the case strictly from the point of view of opposing counsel. What weaknesses would you pursue? What flaws might bear fruit if the worker is questioned? What gaps can you see that need to be filled in?

Participants are often surprised at the volume of queries that arise when a case is considered from the opposing perspective. There is *always* an opposing perspective, but it is seldom explored by those on the agency side. At some point in your case conferences, consider mandating someone to play the role of challenging the operating premises of the conference. Better that the validity of premises be tested prior to court than in court for the first time.

PROVABLE FACTS: THE YELLOW HIGHLIGHTER TEST

Your case notes are the primary record of facts in a case. It is fundamental to your case notes that you be able to review them to identify those facts which would be accepted as evidence in court. It is not necessarily a matter of criticizing the quality of the case notes. Their primary purpose is to inform social worker decisions, which requires a net that catches information well beyond the provable facts alone.

Reviewing the case notes for court purposes is a distinct and separate task. A good review of your case notes will result in your developing a list of the points you will cover on the witness stand, as well as flagging those points which will not be acceptable to a court of law.

Consider the following example of case notes:

Feb. 10 Mary and John Smith visited with their child today.
Next visit in a week's time.
Served notice of permanent wardship. They said they would contest it.

Feb. 17 Smiths came fifteen minutes late for their visit today.
Visit was like being a zoo, child lied and her parents browbeat her about it. Her parents talked to her about things inappropriate for a seven year old to handle, eg., seeing her grandparents.

Feb. 22 Met with both sets of maternal grandparents.
Both sets quite fearful of John, citing repercussions as the most frightening to them.
Both grandparents gave background information on Mary and John.
The most common complaint was John's violence and his aggressive behavior towards Mary, their use of drugs, constant moving about and the unsteadiness of their lifestyle.

Feb. 23 Smiths came to the office to pick up their assistance cheque.
Spoke to them *about what occurs in the visits and the inappropriateness of it.*
Agreed with me and said they would watch it.
Parents requested no visiting take place between child and grand-father Davis. I agreed.

Feb. 24 Smith visit today.
Parents came half an hour late to visit, claiming they had run out gas in the park.
The visit was quite pleasant and parents adhered to our conversation yesterday. They spoke to the child as a child and when one would slip, the other would remind each other of it.
John appeared high, perhaps on methadone.

Mar. 3 Mary called today. Her words were slow, jumping back and forth on topics, leading me to suspect she was high on something.

The italicized portions reveal how much of this verbatim excerpt from casenotes is of no use whatever in a court of law. Boiled down, the provable facts to which this worker can testify are:

1. Parents were fifteen minutes late for their first visit.

2. No explanation is recorded for lateness on the first visit; an excuse was offered for the second, but not checked for validity.
3. Mother called, her words were slow, she jumped back and forth on topics.

This is not to say that the remaining case notes do not present a more complete picture of what is going on for out-of-court purposes. The remaining case notes actually present a rather vivid picture. The problem is the complete lack of *provable facts*. The words used do not record facts, but hunches, assumptions, opinions, hearsay, jargon for family dynamics syndromes, and conclusions—none of it acceptable in court!

To be useful in court, we need to know what *was* the child's lie? *How* did the parents browbeat? What was inappropriate about discussing seeing the grandparents? What repercussions were the grandparents afraid of? *How* was John violent or aggressive? What drugs did they use? How often, when? How often did they move? What else was unstable? *Were these allegations put to the parents, and if so, what did they say?*

Notice how the reference to inappropriateness on February 23 builds on the earlier reference on February 10. But we still don't know *what* is inappropriate. Whatever it is, the parents will watch it!

Why don't the parents want the child to see one of the grandparents? What did the worker *observe* that made her conclude that John was high? Was he asked if he was high on anything?

Make a copy of your own case notes and use a yellow highlighter to mark any of the information which is unacceptable for court purposes. You had better be able to make your case on the unmarked portion left over, because that part *is* your case, as far as the court is concerned.

Applying the yellow highlighter test to your casenotes is a primary step in preparing your case and assessing its strength in court. To make the task easier at first, you might want to go through your notes several times, to flag each of the categories of unacceptable evidence separately. These are the items to look for:

Hearsay   Any secondhand information, *other than* statements made to you by the parents themselves.

Opinion   Any opinions or hunches ("he appeared high") as opposed to the facts upon which the opinion is based ("her words were slow, she jumped back and forth on topics").

Jargon   Jargon is shorthand professional language used to crystalize a whole constellation of specific facts. "Risk factors, bonding, ambivalence, co-dependent, passive-aggressive, unstable" are all jargon. The court needs to know what was observed, not how it was interpreted.

Vagueness Vagueness involves using "relative" language; that is, words such as "dirty clothes" which only have a relative meaning at an unknown place on a scale that ranges from outrageously filthy to almost spotless but not quite. "The shirt had dirt on the bottom of the front and around the neck at the back and a greenish sticky substance on the left sleeve" is specific language!

Metaphors Metaphors, including similies ("the visit was like being in a zoo") vividly convey the essence of a situation without saying anything specific or concrete about it.

In summary, case notes need to record the *specific sensory images* of the events referred to, if the life of the child is to be made real in the mind of the judge. It is these specific, concrete observations that are considered the most reliable form of evidence.

Recording events in case notes and assessing the record for court use are distinct but interrelated skills. Make it a permanent court habit to be conscious of the legal quality of your case notes as you make them.

TYPES OF EVIDENCE

There is nothing fancy about most types of evidence submitted in a protection case. The following are listed in order of the frequency with which they are submitted in family court.

Oral Evidence

Testimony, evidence delivered orally from the witness stand, is the mainstay of the family court, which has neither the time nor staff to cope with the voluminous paperwork (pleadings) of higher courts.

Upon being called to the witness stand, the witness is sworn under oath and remains standing or sits down depending on the custom of the court. The consequence of taking the oath is both to improve the general veracity of the evidence, and to enable the court to use the sanction of perjury should falsehoods be established.

Comments made by counsel are not considered evidence at all, nor are comments that a social worker might occasionally be asked to make semi-informally before or after taking the witness stand. Unsworn conversation is not testimonial evidence.

During examination-in-chief counsel calling the witness cannot ask leading questions; that is, questions that imply the answer within them, or invite a mere "yes" or "no" reply. When counsel calling the witness is finished with examination-in-chief, opposing counsel cross-examines, asking as many leading questions as she pleases.

After the examination-in-chief and the cross-examination are completed, counsel calling the witness is prohibited from having a second crack at the can by asking further questions, *unless* they pertain to a new subject raised for the first time on cross-examination.

In formal terms, although counsel ask the questions, it is the judge to whom replies are directed. There is no rigid rule about facing the judge continuously, such as police officers often do, but a witness does no harm by addressing replies to the judge.

Documentary Evidence

Written statements which are sworn under oath and signed by the author of the statements are called "affidavits," though they are seldom used at the family court level of litigation. The authenticity of all other unsworn documents must be established before they may be filed as exhibits in the hearing.

Before filing a portion of your case notes, for example, the authorship of the statements must be verified, as well as the reliability of the record. To establish reliability, questions are asked to establish that a typewritten record has been compared for accuracy to the original notes, and that the original notes were made immediately after or very shortly after the events to which they refer.

Letters, lists of addresses, child care worker summaries, emergency intervention reports, and written agreements between the agency and the parents are all generally accepted forms of documentary evidence, so long as who wrote them and when can be readily proven. (See the next section for discussion of experts' reports specifically.)

If both counsel agree to the filing of a particular piece of paper, the court is entitled to regard the facts referred to in the document as not in dispute. For this reason, sometimes opposing counsel will agree to the filing of something but make clear that certain portions are not accepted as agreed upon facts, or will later be subject to cross-examination of a witness.

Writings of the child or of his parents can be important evidence of the emotional state of the child or his relationship with the family.

Audio and Videotapes

Technology has made available the option of recording interviews with the child on audiotape or videotape. These are also considered forms of "documentary" evidence. Data about when and how the tapes were recorded, and by whom, must be conveyed in order for the court to consider whether such evidence is admissible.

There is wide variation in judicial acceptance of this form of evidence in sexual abuse cases. Interviewing the child on videotape is a highly skilled art, beyond the scope of this book. Great damage is done to the credibility of videotaped interviews when an unskilled interviewer appears to lead or coax the child-witness. It is also critical to credibility that the recorded interview be the first, or one of the very first, that the child has given. When the record shows that a child has been interviewed by a teacher, two police officers, a sexual offence specialist, a psychologist, a play therapist, and a social worker or two, all prior to the subject videotaped interview, the court is increasingly inclined to refuse to see the videotape at all.

The general "best evidence" rule applies to all forms of documentary evidence. That is, if the witness is available to testify in person, and there is no compelling reason why he should not be called to testify, the court should have the benefit of the evidence directly from the witness, rather than via secondary forms of evidence.

Photographs

Pictures are a neglected form of evidence in protection cases. Medical photographs of injuries to a child are often filed as part of a doctor's report, but photographs of other aspects of the case can be more powerful and vivid evidence than if the same aspects were merely described in words.

In a neglect case, for example, much time and effort involved in relating the living conditions of the child can be saved by photographing the rooms of the home, particularly the kitchen and the area where the child is expected to sleep.

To be admissible in court, you must secure the cause-and-effect chain that results in the pictures being produced. Ideally you will take the pictures yourself and bring them to court. This way you are the only one necessary to properly identify the pictures. Otherwise it may be necessary to call as witnesses the photographer, the developer, and anyone else who had possession of the evidence between the point in time when they were taken and the time they are ultimately presented to the court.

Notice the meticulous practice of medical photographers to ensure that at least one photograph is taken of the whole child, such that identification of the child from pictures of limbs only is not made an issue. If you take close-ups of the inside of a refrigerator in a home, for example, or a bathroom sink, make sure that a picture of the whole kitchen or the whole bathroom is included so there is no question of the identification of the closeup.

"Real" Evidence

This form of evidence refers to actual, physical objects filed as exhibits in the case. "Real" evidence is seldom presented to the court, but it should be more often.

A foster mother may be able to describe a child's nightmares, for example, but her description of the child kicking in the bed to the point of ripping the sheets will not be as compelling as presenting the sheets themselves and asking that they be filed as an exhibit.

When destructive acting-out behavior is noted with toys, consider bringing the damaged toys to court.

Notice the possibilities for real evidence as you go along. Make sure items you think would effectively present the child's life situation don't get lost in the shuffle. Then consult your counsel about real evidence as part of preparing your case for court.

EXPERT EVIDENCE: HARD SCIENCE AND SOFT SCIENCE

The evidence of experts is an important source of assistance to courts in understanding how families work. The general rule is that the evidence of expert witnesses will be admitted in court *when the subject matter of the inquiry is such that ordinary people are unlikely to form a correct judgment about it, if unassisted by persons with special knowledge.* In weighing the likely impact of the expert you propose to call, it is useful to make a distinction between "hard science" experts and "soft science" experts.

These terms are not used in court, but they are a way of underscoring the preference of the legal system for objective facts. There is no judicial hesitation to accept necessary "hard science" evidence, such as that of a doctor testifying to the results of a medical examination. A fracture is a fracture, a bruise is a bruise, and expert testimony including opinions about probable causes of such injuries is widely accepted as having a solid empirical basis.

Expertise in the "softer" sciences of psychology, particularly regarding child abuse issues, is not so readily accepted. The reason for judicial reluctance is that the soft sciences are not based on readily accepted standards of empirical evidence. When experts testify about about the reliability of statements made by the child, or the propensity of a parent to abuse a child, such opinions do not present the same degree of certainty that most other scientific opinion does.

Indeed, disagreements among experts themselves in this relatively new field is widespread, so the court is entitled to be more reluctant to accept such evidence at face value.

In some cases the court will consider that the evidence of the particular expert offends the general rule cited above, in that an ordinary person (such as the judge himself) may be regarded as quite as able as an expert to hear the evidence in the case and make a correct judgment about whether the child is at risk.

If common sense can serve to interpret events reasonably well, expert opinion is unnecessary. There is also the fact that psychology, long regarded as the black sheep, the "pseudo-science" in the family of sciences, occasionally exposes a predisposition to the view that "if you can measure it, it must mean something." The court is vigilant to ensure that harmless facts are not interpreted to confirm preconceived but unproven theories.

As always, however, the credibility of the witness is of overriding importance. Imprecise medical evidence will not impress the court just because it is "scientific." Careful, persuasive psychological evidence will not be rejected just because it derives from the art of studying human behavior.

Expert's Reports

As an expert witness is entitled to express opinion based on expertise, there are special formalities involved in calling such a witness to testify. The parents and their counsel are entitled to advance warning of what the expert is going to say, by way of a written summary of the expert's opinion.

Ensure that you know what the formal notice requirements for expert evidence are in your own jurisdiction. A failure to get a copy of the expert's report into the hands of the parents' counsel within the statutory time limit will mean that you will be prevented from calling the expert as a witness. The parents and their counsel have a right to advance consideration of the expert's views, and to decide if they wish to call their own expert in rebuttal.

You need to make an assessment of the quality of the expert's written report prior to going to court. One test is to review the report to see how the expert describes the facts upon which her opinion is based. The weight or value of the opinion is very much affected by what facts have been considered by the expert in arriving at it.

For example, experts are frequently given access to a variety of written reports, case notes, and other documentation to orient them to the case. Opinions based on this sort of information are not given as much weight in court, since the information is all secondhand and not part of the expert's direct observations. Interviews with the family members, on the other hand, produce factual observations to which the expert can testify directly as the foundation of her opinion.

The best written reports of experts state the expert's opinion based on the expert's direct observations, and go on to state further opinions on the explicit assumption that the secondary information examined by the expert is correct. Poorly drafted written reports do not identify the source of information on which the opinion is based, or do not distinguish which parts of the opinion are based on direct observation and which are, in effect, based on hearsay.

Another perspective to assess the value of the expert's evidence is to note the thoroughness of contact with the family. A strong opinion based on one or two brief interviews may be given far less weight than a more moderate opinion following extensive interviews. An expert who interviews the child but does not interview the parent treads dangerous waters if she then expresses opinions concerning the child's relationship with the parent. Opinions about family relationships are much weakened if all family members are not interviewed.

There is a natural tendency to defer to expertise. This tendency can create a false sense of security in a protection case. If you are involved in a case that rests primarily on a strong expert's report, review the strength of this evidence with your counsel. You may have less evidence than meets the eye.

Qualifying Experts

Any legally competent person can be called to court to testify about what has been observed, but experts must be "qualified" in court before they are permitted to express opinions. This means that the court must be satisfied that the witness has special knowledge sufficient to entitle her to express an opinion.

The first step in qualifying an expert witness is to define for the court the specific area of expertise in which the expert's opinion is sought. When this is agreed upon, the effect is to define the parameters of the expert's evidence—the expert is not entitled to present additional opinions outside the area of expertise for which she is called.

The second step is to present the expert's credentials, usually in the form of a resume reciting the expert's academic training and professional experience. It is only after the area of expertise has been defined and the expert's credentials have been accepted by the court that the expert can address the issues in the case.

As mentioned earlier, a fact proven in court must be accepted by the judge. Opinion evidence stands on a different footing altogether. The judge is entitled to assign what weight he chooses to the expert's opinion, or to disregard it entirely. It is, after all, only an opinion, not a fact.

Due to this judicial discretion, initial skirmishes involving challenges to the qualifications of the expert are often red herrings. The court will be more inclined to qualify the expert and hear what she has to say, knowing that the opinion can be assigned no weight at all, than to accept arguments that would prevent her from testifying in the first place. In the same vein, at the conclusion of the case opposing counsel can always argue that an unfavorable expert opinion should be assigned little or no weight. Indeed, how much weight should properly be assigned to expert evidence is an issue in every case in which experts are called.

Reluctant Experts

Before engaging an expert for assistance in a court case, become familiar with your local protocols for dealing with experts. Unless the expert is employed directly by your agency for the purpose of providing court testimony, experts are entitled to bill for their services, which include interviewing parties, preparing a written report, and attending court. Be clear about how these costs will be dealt with. Often special arrangements are made for experts in protection cases to provide services at rates well below those available to them in private practice. Make sure your experts are aware of any fee limits and agree to them before the engagement begins.

Some experts are willing to provide assessment or therapy to family members, but do not want to testify in court. Witnesses can be compelled to testify, but a hostile witness does your case little good. When arranging for assessment or therapeutic services, consider the likelihood that the expert may need to be called into court later on. Determine the expert's willingness to testify before engaging her, and consult your counsel if you see problems on the horizon.

Consulting with Your Counsel

You need to consult with your counsel whenever you intend to call an expert witness. This is particularly important since the court has no obligation to accept the opinions of experts, which evidence, after all, is merely tendered to assist the court in determining the truth. Opinions are not facts. Much depends on the credibility of the particular witness, and your counsel can assist you in assessing credibility both before court and during trial as the testimony proceeds.

Your counsel can also assist you in identifying any gaps or weaknesses in the expert's report, which will give you a handle on both the credibility of the evidence and the areas of likely attack by opposing counsel. Expert evidence can do much to assist the court to understand what is happening in the family, but every case ultimately depends upon the foundation of proven facts.

Chapter 7

COURT:
THE BUCK STOPS HERE

DISCRETION AND ACCOUNTABILITY

Out in the field you represent the duty of the state to assist families and protect children. The services you are mandated to provide are specified in legislation and regulations, and methods of service are defined in the policies of the agency employing you. Within this framework the decisions you make are largely discretionary.

You make judgment calls every day about what services to offer, and when, and how. You can influence, persuade, admonish, tempt, and motivate. But fundamentally your mandate is to work *with* the family, assisting them to resolve problems voluntarily. You are accountable to your supervisor and your agency, and perhaps the parents have the right to have your decisions reviewed. How successful you are depends mainly upon how well you exercise the discretion vested in you.

Once a child is removed from the family because you consider him at risk, the legal system becomes the primary vehicle requiring both you and the parents to be accountable for your actions. The act of removal escalates what is at stake on both sides: you must justify your actions based on provable facts, not mere discretion, and the parents are now subject to the power of the court to *compel* results rather than merely encouraging them.

As with any system designed to deal with problems of human behavior, both the legal system and the agency are subject to debate about their respective effectiveness, priorities, efficiency, and fairness. A separate line of debate surrounds the statutory attempts to define the circumstances in which the state is justified in intervening in private family affairs, as discussed in Chapter 5. Participation in these debates is a part of your right and even obligation as a social worker.

But the court is not the forum for debate about these issues, at least on your part.

To be effective in court you need to accept the validity of the court's mandate to hold you accountable. It is easy to become so involved in a case that other decisionmakers are seen in terms of interference. Notice the presence of this attitude as you go to court. Its presence is a solid indicator that you may need to reconceptualize the role of the court in your work.

You may find it helpful to identify the courtroom door as the place where the formal shift in power takes place. Prior to reaching the courtroom door, you may encourage, persuade, and advocate as you see fit, as the mantle of responsibility for the child rests solely upon your shoulders. Once you have removed the child, however, the mantle of responsibility is no longer yours, alone. When you pass through the courtroom door, you need to shift your professional focus to the new task of making the life of the child real for the judge. It is now the judge who bears ultimate responsibility for the fate of the child.

Signs that a worker has made the appropriate shift in professional focus include an evenhandedness in testimony, a willingness to give credit to the parents, an obvious intention to present *all* the facts, a patent fairness in manner and conduct, and a fundamental neutrality, in the sense of leaving it to the court to make the decision it is mandated to make.

Signs that a worker is possessive of the case and resistant to accepting the authority of the court include an emphasis on the dark side of the family picture, a resistance to give any credit to the parents, a tone of resentment at having to testify at all, an unwillingness to share information about the case, and a fundamental adversarialness.

An incidental but important difference between these two choices is that the worker who "shifts gears" at the courtroom door tends to proceed through the court process calmly; she is not personally at stake. The worker who clings to responsibility for the result in the case tends to experience court process as stressful; she "fails" if the court decides the application is unwarranted.

HONORING SOLOMON

The task of deciding the fate of an abused or neglected child is no easier for the judge than it is for you. In many ways the judge's task is more difficult. He cannot consider the whole range of information available about the family, but only those aspects you present, and then only if that information conforms to restrictive evidentiary rules designed to ensure that legal decisions are made on the basis of provable facts.

The judge is also at least as aware as you are that neither choosing to return the child home nor placing him in state care amounts to an ideal solution.

Wouldn't it be nice if someone could wave a magic wand and guarantee the child not only safety and minimal care, but also love and warmth and support, such that the child could achieve the best that he could be? The judge can't guarantee these results, and neither can you.

All the judge can do is make the best decision among the choices available, based on the information he is permitted to consider. Like you, the judge is doing the best he can.

Furthermore, like you, the judge must live with the results of his choices. A bad decision is his responsibility alone; there is no agency or chain of command in which to spread the blame. Mistakes are made. Children are injured or even die. The burden of being responsible to choose is not a light one.

Notice your attitude to the judge and his role. You and he are both professionals, entitled to honor for having embraced difficult and unpopular tasks. You each operate by different rules and belief systems and make decisions by different methods, but each of you has also elected to invest your energies for the same purpose: to protect children. The honor and respect you display will tend to be reflected in the honor and respect you receive.

THE JUDICIAL SKEPTIC

Occasionally you may encounter judicial skepticism about what you have to say in court. Judges are trained to be skeptical, of course, in the sense of seeking convincing proof of allegations. But sometimes, with a particular judge or with a particular case, it may seem that the judge is critical of every single decision you have made and suspicious of everything you say.

There are two possible scenarios which explain this experience.

The least probable is that you are faced with a very cranky judge who doesn't like you and doesn't believe you. Once in awhile this may be the case. Some judges are not suited to family court just as some social workers are not suited to protection work. Judges experience burnout, as do social workers. Some judges develop a jaundiced view of the agency's effect on families. Some consider that they are the only ones in the system capable of making competent decisions.

If you encounter a very cranky judge, rely on your professionalism. Do not engage in argument. Do not buy into the criticism game offered. Focus on the child before the court and allow gratuitous comment to run off your back, as you would in the field. Before you reach court, consciously choose your techniques for moving through the court process, to reduce the risk of reacting personally. There are good days and bad days to any job.

The more probable scenario to explain why you seem to be constantly criticized in court involves poor preparation and presentation, or both. Before deciding too quickly that the issue has to do with the particular judge, review the basics of your approach to court.

Review Chapter 1: have you accommodated the judge's need for specific sensory information or have you lapsed into professional jargon? Review Chapter 2: have you been frank and evenhanded with the parents, or does your conduct appear coercive and manipulative? Review Chapter 3: have you followed a conscious protocol to present the case effectively in court, or do you appear to be flying by the seat of your pants? Review Chapter 4: do you know what your strengths and weaknesses are, or are your weaknesses only apparent to the judge? Review Chapter 5: have you been careful in observing the proprieties of your protection statute, or are you hoping the court will fill in the gaps? Review Chapter 6: have you demonstrated a professional understanding of what evidence is, or have you left it to other players to get a grip on your case?

Criticism from the bench is important information. It may indicate no more than that the judge got out of the wrong side of the bed, but it is more likely to indicate that some aspects of your preparation or presentation simply do not meet the standards required by the court to enable it to do its job. Judicial skepticism about the allegations in the case is normal and goes with the territory. Where the skepticism is pervasive and overflows to the point of criticism, it may be an invitation to review your approach. If you have reviewed your approach and conclude you are handling yourself properly, let unwarranted criticism wash away and forget about it.

THE OTHER PLAYERS IN COURT

Family court is a stage involving other actors besides the judge and yourself. At the entrance to the courtroom stands the sheriff, responsible for calling the cases. The court recorder and the court clerk sit between the bench where the judge is seated and the counsel table. The recorder maintains the official record of the proceeding. Usually this is done by tape recording, with the recorder noting occasional words and phrases and cross-referencing them by number with the point on the tape where they occur.

Should you or your counsel require a transcript of the proceeding later on, this is prepared from the tape recording. You may also have access to the tape itself, should you wish to hear a portion of a hearing but not require a transcript. Find out what kind of access you are permitted to the official court record.

The court clerk, who in some courts calls the cases in lieu of the sheriff, is the documentary gatekeeper for the judge and the official court file. A document to be filed as an exhibit is not passed directly to the judge, but through the court clerk. If the judge accepts the document as a proper exhibit in the case, it is handed back to the clerk to be stamped and placed in the court file.

Family courts are less formal physically than superior courts, but counsel sit separately from their clients. On some cases the parents may be unrepresented by counsel, and your counsel will be the only lawyer in the courtroom. On others each of the parties may be represented and counsel may be appointed to represent the child as well. In an unusual case there may be separate counsel for yourself, the child, the separated mother, the separated father, a separated step-parent, a caretaking relative, and a native band—seven lawyers in all!

The parties to the proceeding are entitled to remain in the courtroom throughout the hearing. At a minimum, this means yourself as the representative of the agency, and the parents.

Witnesses are treated differently (other than yourself and the parents). In a contested hearing numerous witnesses may be called by each side. Your counsel will call his witnesses first, who will be examined by him and then cross-examined by all opposing counsel. Then opposing counsel will call her witnesses for examination-in-chief, and each of these will be cross-examined in turn by your counsel. Witnesses are not entitled to be in the courtroom during other testimony, which ensures that one witness' testimony will not be influenced by hearing that of another.

At the conclusion of the case each counsel makes a "submission" or argument to the court about how the evidence should be weighed and how the law applies. The submissions of counsel do not constitute evidence, as counsel are not sworn under oath or witnesses in the case. They are merely arguments intended to persuade the court to the point of view of each counsel's client. The judge may find assistance in counsel's submissions about the evidence, but he may also disregard submissions entirely if he sees fit.

The judge can give his decision on the spot, either making his order and leaving it at that, or provide oral reasons to explain how he viewed the evidence and how he arrived at his decision. In difficult cases, particularly if an unusual point of law is raised, the judge may "reserve" his decision. This means he wishes to take time to ponder the case and will render his decision on a later date, often providing written reasons for judgment and reading them into the record at that time.

Protection cases can proceed by consent, or unopposed, or opposed. There may be many witnesses, or only yourself. There may be one counsel or several. However large or small the case, the same basic steps are followed, even if the whole hearing takes only a few minutes.

WHO NEEDS LAWYERS?

Some jurisdictions have experimented with protection applications being made by social workers directly, at least in unopposed matters or straightforward applications to deal with problems in serving documents. Historically social workers in many jurisdictions handled all but the most protracted cases directly.

The argument in favor of keeping lawyers out of protection cases has to do with the adversarial factor that lawyers are seen to bring to family cases. The argument in favor of involving lawyers at the outset is that there is a greater assurance that the legal rights of parents will be protected, and that the facts of the case will have a complete airing, fully tested by cross-examination. The presence of lawyers also tends to ensure due process is complied with, as lawyers are trained to protect their clients' rights to a fair hearing.

Some lawyers take an aggressive adversarial position at the outset of any case, regardless of the situation. Experience with such lawyers increases the tendency to see lawyers as more of a hindrance than a help to families in conflict.

In the main lawyers who are drawn to protection work, whether they represent the agency or the parents, tend to acknowledge the value of negotiation and other nonadversarial approaches to achieving the goals of their clients. For the line social worker the presence of the agency lawyer in court means that the burden of the court process is a shared burden. How much of an ally the agency lawyer is to the social worker is primarily a function of the working relationship between the two, which itself is a function of how much energy has been invested in mutual clarification of the roles and expectations.

In a few jurisdictions protection cases are dealt with by nonlegal community panels, in an attempt to remove the adversarial factor and to focus on the investigatory rather than the adjudicative purpose of a protection hearing. These experimental alternatives have not been widespread. As parents become increasingly forceful in asserting their full legal rights, it becomes less and less likely that the court system will be replaced as the forum of final decision in protection matters.

WHY COURT AT ALL: POLICY AND POLITICS

Historically the courts have evolved as the civilized alternative to the otherwise potentially violent resolution of disputes. Society acknowledges that when disputes arise, *someone* has to make the final decision. Judges, with their familiarity with rules of due process and with their orientation to provable objective evidence, are seen as neutral bystanders vested with authority to make binding decisions for others, by virtue of their training and experience.

The majority of social services are effectively provided without involvement of the court system. When voluntary efforts ultimately fail, the court system becomes available to ensure that decisions about families in crisis are made in a manner that requires the agency to account for its actions and provides the parents with the opportunity to have their side of the story heard by someone who is both independent and empowered with full authority to make decisions.

As a policy matter it may well be that protection cases should be dealt with by alternatives to the court system. It remains for society to establish alternatives which both protect the rights of all parties and resolve matters with less delay, hostility, and confusion than occurs at times under the present system. Convincing alternatives have yet to be created.

There is also a political factor mitigating against removing protection cases from the court system. The problem of abuse and neglect of children can be examined from the narrowest perspective of the particular family and the particular child, up to the broadest perspective of social policy relating to the great social issues of the day. The problems of poverty, unemployment, marital violence, substance abuse and emotional deprivation are factors in the vast majority of abuse and neglect cases. None of these issues admits of easy political solution. In the absence of courageous leadership, the safest political route is to avoid the hornet's nest wherever possible.

Since the legal system is oriented to define specific issues in specific cases and has no mandate to address policy or politics directly, the relative silence of the players most familiar with the problems is ensured. The legal system makes the necessary final decisions in specific cases, but the players in the system cannot use the court as a forum to address the larger social issues at stake. The rather incongruous result is that although the social consciousness about the gravity and extent of child abuse and neglect in society has increased dramatically, the frontline players directly involved—social workers, protection lawyers, and judges—are professionally discouraged from using actual cases to speaking out publically on the larger issues.

While public commentators grapple with the complex problem of why we hurt and neglect our children to the extent we do, and sometimes pass the buck of responsibility from one arena to another, there remains an ongoing need to make final decisions in actual family situations. For that given family and that particular child, the buck stops in court.

Chapter 8

IN THE TRENCHES:
ASSESSING THE STRENGTH OF YOUR CASE

NAILING DOWN THE ISSUES

The ultimate legal issue in every protection case may be stated as follows: "Was the child abused or neglected at the time he was removed from the home?" That is, to obtain an order protecting the child, you must be able to provide the court with sufficient convincing evidence that enables it to respond to the ultimate legal issue in the affirmative: "Yes, the child was abused or neglected at the time he was removed from the home." This "finding" of abuse or neglect is the jurisdictional basis for the court moving on to the "dispositional" phase of the hearing and granting a specific protection order.

A common omission in assessing the strength of a protection case is to omit the identification of the legal issues which the court must decide. Whether or not a child is abused or neglected does not depend upon the personal views of yourself, the judge, or the lawyers as to what conduct amounts to abuse or neglect. It depends upon how these terms are defined in your protection statute, as refined by case decisions in your jurisdiction.

Even in the most straightforward interventions, those that are likely to result in a summary disposition in court, the legal issues need to be nailed down. For example, where a child is left alone by the parents and is removed from the home as a result, the broad issue is whether such parental conduct is sufficiently reckless to justify a court finding that the child was neglected. This broad issue can be broken down into several narrower legal issues to be decided by the court:

1. Was the child of an age such that leaving him home alone was unsafe?
2. Regardless of age, did *this particular child* lack sufficient maturity to cope safely with being on his own?
3. Did the parents make adequate caretaking arrangements for the

child, and if they did, what happened to cause these arrangements to fall through? Can the cause for the breakdown of arrangements be laid at the feet of the parents or did external factors enter into the picture?

4. Was the length of time that the child was left alone unreasonable and unsafe under the circumstances?
5. Who else was in the home at the time?
6. Did the child know where the parents were and did he have the ability to contact them if necessary?
7. Was the reason for the absence of the parent reasonable in itself; that is, were the parents away for reasons other than related family problems such as alcohol abuse which would suggest a parental difficulty in putting the needs of the child ahead of adult needs?
8. Is there a history of similar breakdowns of caretaking or is this an isolated incident?

The bald *fact* of leaving a child alone is not necessarily neglect in and of itself. Defining the legal questions which put this fact into the context of the living experience of the family enables the court to weigh the gravity of the bald fact against the legal standard of minimal parental care which parents are obliged to provide.

Framing the issues is not an esoteric or complicated art. To identify the issues in your own case, simply take a detached view of the situation for a few moments, and list all the questions which might reasonably be asked about different aspects of the incident. Many of these questions will constitute the legal issues in the case.

In a case in which abuse is alleged as a result of physical injury to the child, the broad legal issue of whether the physical treatment of the child by the parents constitutes abuse may be broken down into several narrower legal questions to be decided by the court, as well:

1. Is there evidence of the nature and extent of the injury?
2. Do the parents have a satisfactory explanation of the injury?
3. Does the nature and extent of the injury arguably fall within the right of parents to physically discipline their children?
4. What is the context of the incident? That is, what was the behavior of the child that "triggered" the physical response of the parent, if any? Provocation by a child does not justify abuse, but the degree of risk to the child cannot be assessed without facts about the nature of the parent-child conflict.

5. How appropriate was the degree of physical force used in light of the age of the child?
6. Is there a history of previous problems with physical injury to the child?
7. Is there a history of previous problems with physical injury to other children in the family?

The above lists of issues to be determined by the court are not intended as general prescriptions for every case, or even as exhaustive for the "straightforward" examples mentioned of a child left alone or a child who is injured. They are intended to suggest the manner in which the court is obliged to *approach* the case, by defining the questions that need to be answered in order to assign a proper weight to the conduct alleged, to put that conduct into the real-life context of the family in which the child actually lives, and to enable the court to decide whether that conduct amounts to abuse or neglect *as defined* by the protection statute.

There are three main advantages to beginning your assessment of the strength of your case by defining the issues which the court needs to decide.

First, framing the case in terms of the issues at stake immediately enables you to consider the case in the manner that the legal system considers it, as opposed to how you and your colleagues may see the family from a purely social work perspective. Every type of legal case presents the court with questions to be answered. Every lawyer is expected to define for the court what questions the court is being asked to decide. Defining these questions yourself at the outset is the quickest way to grasp the court process involved.

Second, even "simple" cases involve a series of questions that need to be defined and answered. In any case, but especially in complicated ones, it is easy to become overwhelmed by the sea of details and swayed by dramatic incident to the point of losing sight of the step-by-step process the court must go through. The wealth of details can rapidly become unwieldy and confusing; identifying the issues enables a more realistic vision of "what the case is about."

Third, an identification of the issues at stake allows you to proceed to categorize the evidence you have available under each of the issues. If you have identified the issues correctly, assembling the provable evidence you have relating to each question will quickly reveal the strengths and weaknesses of your case. You may wish to consult with your counsel once you have identified the issues, to see if there are other issues you should consider, and to get a sense of where your case falls in relation to the elusive dividing line between minimally acceptable parental behavior and conduct which legally constitutes abuse or neglect.

NAILING DOWN THE FACTS

Legally speaking, your views of the family situation that resulted in your intervention merely amount to allegations until you prove the facts in a court of law. The critical point to note is that whether specific facts in the case are treated by the court as "convincing proof" or "irrelevant or inadmissible" depends primarily upon how you go about collecting the evidence and how you present it.

Presenting factual evidence in court requires a working familiarity with how truth is established in a court of law. Review Chapter 6 if you are uncertain about what categories of evidence are acceptable to a court and how facts should be presented.

Of paramount importance is nailing down the facts surrounding the intervention incident itself. The evidence relating to the issues which will put the incident into context for the court are important, but if you do not have convincing proof that the facts justify the original act of intervention, the court will be obliged to order the child returned home.

Nailing down the facts surrounding the removal of the child amounts to asking, "What do we know and how do we know it?" Consider the following sources of information about the intervention incident itself:

1. Your own direct observations of the event, assuming you were present at the intervention;
2. The observations of any other witnesses present at the intervention;
3. Admissions made to you by either of the parents at the time (which should be recorded verbatim);
4. Photographs taken at the home, or photographs taken of the child immediately after apprehension by a medical photographer;
5. The medical report on the child, and the testimony of the doctor who made the report;
6. Physical evidence, being actual objects relevant to the incident resulting in the intervention;
7. Statements made to you by the child, assuming such statements

are admissible as an exception to the rule against hearsay in your jurisdiction;

8. The testimony and reports of any experts retained to provide expert opinion about the intervention to assist the court.

In addition to the above sources of information about the intervention incident itself, supplementary sources of information which assist the court by placing the intervention in the context of your history of involvement with the family include:

9. The formal history of prior protection proceedings regarding the subject child or any of his siblings;
10. The history of any agreements entered into between the parents and your agency;
11. Your observations made during home visits prior to and subsequent to the intervention;
12. The testimony of other witnesses involved with the family, such as homemakers, child guidance counsellors, school teachers, school counsellors, neighbors, police officers, the family doctor, psychologists, and psychiatrists, including any admissions made by the parents to any of these witnesses;
13. The testimony of the foster parents as to the behavior of the child and regarding visits with the parents, if the child has been placed in foster care following the intervention;
14. The testimony of witnesses called by the parents.

These examples of sources of information are not intended to be exhaustive. Protection cases vary widely in their circumstances and complexity. It is part of your task in assessing the strength of your case to identify the sources of available information.

It is useful to distinguish between "intervention" sources of information, which provide direct evidence about the incident resulting in the removal of the child, and "context" sources of information, which give the court broader information about the life of the family. Sometimes there is so much context information that there is a tendency to gloss over the fact of the intervention itself. The context information is ultimately irrelevant if sufficient evidence has not been collected to convince the court that the child was at risk at the time of the intervention.

When you have identified the intervention sources of information, you can relate this evidence to the list of issues you have identified earlier. This capsule summary of the case, with the issues identified and the evidence related to those issues, enables you to make an assessment of whether you will be likely to convince the court that the intervention was justified. At this point you may wish to present your capsule summary to your counsel to obtain his opinion about the intervention phase of the case.

When you have identified the context sources of information and related these to the issues you have identified in the case, you will be able to make an assessment about the dispositional phase of the case as well. Whether the court finds the child in need of protection depends upon the intervention information, but once the finding is made, the type of order granted depends upon both the intervention information and the context information.

Apart from identifying the various sources of evidence, you will need to make an assessment of its reliability. Your counsel will appreciate your making a summary of the facts to which each witness can testify, but the persuasive power of the testimony depends upon the credibility of each of the witnesses.

You will need to make a summary of the facts to which you can testify yourself so that your counsel can prepare appropriate questions. In reviewing your casenotes, consider the points raised in Chapter 6, especially the "yellow highlighter test."

It is really impossible to assess the strengths and weaknesses of your case unless the issues and the sources of information have been identified. These two steps are the basic components of your preparation for court. They are also distinct court skills, which become easier over time.

BRIEF TO COUNSEL

As part of developing a working relationship with your counsel, you need to determine what type of information he requires prior to an application, and what form he wants it in.

It is up to you to prepare your case and determine the evidence you have to support your application. It is also up to you to "translate" this evidence into a form which will enable your counsel to represent you properly. It is not counsel's job to sift through your casenotes and help you decide whether you have a case at all. It is up to you to decide what Order you want to apply for and to identify what facts you have to support your application. Your counsel can then advise you how well those facts support your application.

Your written summary of the case is often referred to as your "Brief to

Counsel." There is no special format for a written brief. The point is that you need to brief your counsel in the sense of providing him with a written summary of the case particulars, the specific points of evidence you want to make in your testimony, and the type of Order and terms you seek.

On an unopposed or consent application you may require little or no consultation time with your counsel, or perhaps just a telephone conference. Even if it seems unnecessary, a short conference or phone call will often generate questions of detail which can be resolved so that the court application proceeds as smoothly as possible.

There are no rules about the amount of counsel time you are "entitled" to, so it's up to you and your counsel to establish your own practice. If you are feeling nervous about the application for some reason and want a thorough conference about the case with your counsel, you are fully entitled to arrange one. You can also use this time to get clarification about court process and pointers about how to handle yourself in court, if you wish. But remember, counsel are just as busy as you are, and you would do well to present yourself as prepared as possible to go to court. Your counsel doesn't have the time to put your case together for you, nor is that his job. If you simply present yourself in a state of panic with a chaotic file of documents, your counsel is unlikely to offer you therapy or tea—more than likely, he will tell you to bring the mess to court and let you sort yourself out in front of the judge! On the other hand, if you have done your best and need help with specific questions, most counsel will tend to bend over backwards, a posture that becomes more familiar as they spend years in court.

A contested trial may last anywhere from half a day to a monstrous ten days or more, interspersed by perhaps weeks of adjournments. There is usually only one opposing counsel but there may be as many as three or more. In rare cases a family advocate may be appointed to represent the child. Once the contested hearing has commenced with the hearing of evidence, the judge in question will consider himself "seized" of the case, and will remain on the case to the end.

Speaking very broadly, contested abuse cases will involve evidence focused narrowly on a few specific events. Contested neglect cases involve a much larger quantity of much less dramatic events, as there may be much history to the case and the real issue in dispute is often whether the whole pattern of events "adds up" to the point that the child is at risk.

Your first step in preparing your Brief to Counsel should be to review your own case notes from a legal perspective. For the purposes of this discussion, let's take it as a given that your sense about what has happened and your intuition and judgment about the level of risk and what needs to be done is completely accurate and sound. In fact it is these skills, the talents for perception, intuition, and judgment, which are really fundamental to your working effectively with families in crisis.

That said, don't be offended to learn that these talents may actually work against you in preparing your case for court. As discussed earlier, the court process is the legislated "check-and-balance" to those talents of yours, and to your enormous discretionary powers. Accordingly, the whole set of rules for making decisions alters once court process is involved. What counts in court are the facts you can *prove* to be true. Use the yellow highlighter test described in Chapter 6 to distinguish the wheat from the chaff in your case notes.

In fact, you can use any approach to assessing your case notes that will assist you in making a judgment about how much provable fact they contain. The point is that rules against hearsay and opinion and the legal orientation to specificity of language operate as "first stage filters" in a court process which, by definition, is mandated to make protection decisions based on facts provable in court.

Case notes are not, by themselves, briefs to counsel. Indeed, assessing how solid your notes are from a legal perspective is a major aspect of your skill in making case notes as you go along. The social worker who does not make this assessment may also be unaware that the contents of case notes are subject to legal filters—they aren't "evidence" just because they're in the file.

(This is not to say that case notes should contain nothing but provable facts. The type of information a worker is entitled to collect and rely on in assisting the family is far broader than the type of information the judge can permit himself to consider. But where the notes do refer to information to be tendered in court, such information must contain *specific sensory images* of the events referred to, if the life of the child is to be made real in the mind of the judge. It is the specific, concrete observations, after all, that will be regarded as the most reliable type of evidence about the child's situation.)

After you have "tested" your case notes to see how much provable information they contain, how should you organize the information in anticipation of briefing your counsel and testifying in court?

Set your notes aside and consider your case in general. Make a list of the events which have occurred that you feel would support a finding that the child was in need of protection. Then refer back to your case notes, to the provable facts *only,* to extract those facts which amount to proof of the various events on your list. Any important event on your list which does not have supporting provable facts to support it is a weak spot in your case.

You will be able to prove some events from the facts in your case notes alone. When you have identified these, you will have identified the points of your own testimony in court. Other events will require other forms of supporting evidence or the testimony of other witnesses. When you have identified these, you will have identified the points of evidence of your other witnesses and relevant reports.

If important events remain which are not supported by your case notes or the testimony or reports of others, you will have nailed down the gaps in your case. Putting this whole process in written form will result in the creation of your brief to your counsel as well as self-preparation for testifying.

Don't omit "real" evidence from your brief, if there is any available. Besides talking about what happened (testimony) or rendering facts in writing (documentary evidence), there may be actual objects—"real" evidence—which you may wish to identify as relevant to the case and accordingly bring to court.

"Real" or physical evidence is a rather neglected area in protection cases. Your success in conveying the "sensory images" of the case to the judge in court is a function of your flair for verbal description. Much is to be gained by adding to the words an actual, physical remnant of the incident itself. If the mother slaps the child for wearing a blouse the mother considers too low-cut, bring in the blouse and let the judge see it for himself. If there was a knife in an incident, bring in the knife.

"Real" evidence is part of the event. At only one remove from the event is the photograph of it. Pictures can convey the reality of the child's experience with a vividness seldom captured easily in words. Broken glass, bottles lying around, a near-empty fridge, a kitchen in total disarray—these are elements of the child's experience which can be conveyed more powerfully by photographs than testimony. Photographs of injuries are in a special category of their own, in that no words can convey damage to a child with the same impact as a photograph. You can take the judge to the home with pictures, let him look inside the fridge, see the broken window, the mess. Note the date and time the pictures were taken.

Not every case benefits from "real" or photographic evidence, but assessing your evidence also includes deciding the best form in which to submit it. If you intend to present these categories of evidence, list them on your Brief to Counsel.

In cases where numerous witnesses may be called, you will need to consult your counsel early to determine how their evidence is to be handled. It is your case, so you are expected to provide your counsel with at least a summary in point form of what evidence each witness has to offer.

Find out from your counsel whether you are to handle arranging for subpoenas to be issued to the witnesses by dealing with court directly, or whether he will handle that task. Will your counsel wish to interview the witnesses himself, or will he have queries from your summary that he expects you to follow up by way of interviews? Do you want to discuss the order in which the witnesses will be called? Are there witnesses on your list who your counsel feels aren't required, and are you to let them know or will he do that? Are there witnesses whose evidence is really no more than you can say yourself by way of admissions made to you by the parties?

Numerous witnesses add considerably to the details of presenting the case to court, and if you are not clear about the roles of your counsel and yourself in the task, consult your counsel early. You are responsible for investigating the case and accumulating the evidence, and your counsel is responsible for determining how best to present that evidence in court. Beyond that there are no hard and fast rules about how the responsibilities are to mesh in the particular case, so you will need to work things out with your counsel early on.

The starting point is to list the witnesses with a summary of their evidence on your Brief to Counsel, along with the witnesses' addresses and telephone numbers, so your counsel can get a feel for the people involved with the case.

List the experts you intend to call on your Brief to Counsel with their addresses and telephone numbers so that your counsel can contact them if he wishes. Attach written reports of experts to your Brief, or note when you expect to receive them.

If you feel areas of the evidence would be suitable for submission in the form of a Statement of Agreed Upon Facts, identify these in your brief as well.

Your Brief to Counsel is simply a written summary intended assist your counsel in preparing himself to represent the agency effectively in court. The Brief can take any form which suits both you and your counsel. Beyond listing particulars about the child before the court and his siblings and parents, the *goal* of the Brief is to enable your counsel to familiarize himself quickly with the evidence concerning your application, such that he is put in a position of being able to *advise* you about the strengths and weaknesses of the case. Any form of summarizing the material facts which achieves this goal is suitable.

Your counsel is entitled to expect an adequate Brief. It is your job, not his, to assemble the evidence, identify and summarize it, and weigh its strength in the first instance. It is his job to advise you about the evidence in terms of its likely impact in court. Your counsel may well wish to see some or all of your case in its "raw" form, including your case notes, reports, and correspondence, and other records on file. But you are not entitled simply to give your counsel the file and tell him to brief himself.

Your counsel is entitled to expect that the raw data has been professionally filtered and boiled down to meet the criteria of provable evidence submitted to a court of law. The quality of your counsel's representation of your case in court is often directly related to the quality of your Brief. If you appear to your counsel to be disinclined to determine the merits of your case before walking into the court room, your counsel may well adopt the same position.

Due to the time limitations you may wish to give your counsel a "draft" Brief as soon after the initial intervention as possible. If you wait until you have fully and completely investigated the case to prepare your Brief, you may limit its usefulness in terms of your being too late to pursue further lines of inquiry based on your counsel's advice, or in terms of leaving your counsel too little time to pursue settlement negotiations effectively.

THE BURDEN OF PROOF

As mentioned earlier, truth is a mistress of many faces. In protection cases, the court is mandated to determine the truth. The findings of fact made by the court constitute society's "formal truth" of events, regardless of any defects in the findings resulting from the limitations imposed by evidentiary rules or any gaps in presenting the case.

If the court finds as a fact that the father does not have a problem with alcohol, then in formal terms he does not, and there is nothing whatever you can do about your own view to the contrary, barring an appeal based on an error of law. In protection cases, as in all other litigation, at some point society requires that someone make a decision about "what's what," and in our society the court does this job under the protection statute.

Accordingly it is important to acknowledge that, from the court's perspective, the case must be made out on a "balance of probabilities." The burden of proof rests on the agency, which must be able to present persuasive evidence that shows, on balance, that its version of events is most probably the correct one.

In a protection case you are not required to prove that facts are absolutely, undeniably true, beyond any reasonable doubt. Proof "beyond a reasonable doubt" is the highest standard of proof, applicable to criminal cases because the liberty of the individual is at stake. In a criminal case, the state must not only prove beyond a reasonable doubt that the accused is guilty, but it must also disprove any alternate explanation of events offered by the accused in his defence.

In a protection case, you must convince the court "on balance," or "by a preponderance of evidence," or "by convincing evidence," that the events you allege "probably" occurred. These are all phrases sometimes used to describe the burden of proof referred to as the "balance of probabilities" standard of proof. If the evidence presented is not clear and compelling, but rather both the agency's version of events and the parents' version seems equally probable to the judge, he is obliged to find that the agency has not made its case, since the burden of proof has not been discharged.

BRINGING THE CHILD'S REALITY TO COURT

Due to the nature of court process and the competing agendas of the various players in court, there is always a risk in protection cases that attention may shift from the child to the needs and goals of the adults involved. Indeed, it may be a specific tactic on the part of counsel for the parents to emphasize evidence relating to the difficulties experienced by the parents, to draw attention away from what has happened to the child.

Making the child's life real in the mind of the judge is your primary goal in the court process. Consider identifying this as a concrete court skill you seek to develop in every case. Your basic tool is the use of sensory images.

For example, if you say, "The child was uncommunicative during the visit," you *are* relating a unit of information about the child's experience, but in a way that cannot create a specific sensory image in the mind of the judge as to what that experience was. On the other hand, you might say, "During the visit, the child only answered 'yes' or 'no' to questions from his mother. He would not look at her when the questions were asked. He looked down at his feet, or at me, and when the mother tried to hug him, he accepted the hug but did not hug her back." Both forms of testimony convey that the child was uncommunicative, but the latter creates specific images of the event as experienced by the child.

It is the concrete detail of the observation related which creates a "living" image of the child's experience. *Show* what the child has experienced by relating the details you have observed, rather than telling *about* the child. As a professional witness and a skilled observer, you are the gatekeeper to the child's reality. The court cannot know what the child felt unless you make a conscious decision to convey the detail of sensory observations that framed his experience.

CONFERENCING THE CASE

Case conferences prior to court often focus on determining whether there is admissible evidence to support the premises about the family situation. You may wish to use case conferences to assist you in identifying the issues at stake as well. As discussed in Chapter 6, you might also take the opportunity to have someone challenge the premises about the family situation, as they may be challenged in court. The central approach to this is to ask, "Are there other reasonably possible explanations of the events, other than the premise we have accepted up until now?" *What if* the premise is altogether wrong? What does the case look like then?

Another possible use of case conferences is to ask someone to challenge your own evidence as you describe the case. At a minimum, this can reveal the parts of your testimony that may be queried in court, and give you the opportunity to describe the same events in a more effective way, with suggestions from your colleagues.

The case conference can also explicitly evaluate the quality and credibility of likely testimony by other witnesses, including experts. Experts' reports will be in hand, and these can be evaluated critically as discussed in Chapter 6, instead of merely relying on favorable recommendations at the end of the reports.

Consider asking your counsel to attend the case conference. The result of his advice at this point can do much to identify the areas of the case which warrant additional attention before the hearing itself.

CONSULTING YOUR COUNSEL

Your counsel is available for consultation during your investigation as well as during your preparation period prior to the court hearing. You may consult your counsel by telephone or in person, alone, or at a case conference. Counsel can provide legal advice about the strengths and weaknesses of your case, and the likelihood of success of your application.

As you get to know your counsel, consider making the subject of your working relationship together an overt item on your consultation agenda. Your counsel may be discreetly reticent about raising problems that arise as he sees them, but he would welcome a direct invitation from you to discuss the respective roles openly.

As discussed in other sections, it is your responsibility to decide what application to make, to identify the issues at stake and the sources of information to prove the factual basis of the case, and to put the particulars of the evidence of yourself and other witnesses in summary form by way of briefing your counsel. A close working relationship with your counsel will result in case strategy and direction being developed on a consultative basis.

Some workers put little effort into identifying the issues and the sources of information, preferring to leave it to their counsel. Concrete disadvantages result from this approach: the strength of the case is often not discovered until court, the opportunity to identify and fill in the gaps is lost, the working relationship with counsel often becomes impaired, and the very purpose of the intervention—to protect the child—may be defeated.

The best working relationships between social workers and their counsel proceed on the British barrister-solicitor model. The solicitor (social worker) has the responsibility to identify the issues, assemble the evidence, and present summaries of the evidence by way of briefing the barrister. The barrister (agency counsel) has the responsibility to offer advice about the case, decide in what order the evidence should be called, and present the case in court.

When a social worker declines to accept the solicitor role and leaves everything to her counsel, he is not likely to make an issue of it. It is not up to him to define the social worker's responsibilities, and there is a reluctance to be direct about the parameters of the working relationship unless the social worker raises the issue in the first place. Counsel is more likely to approach the case with a lessening enthusiasm. He is, after all, only the "creature of instructions" of the social worker; it is ultimately the social worker's case, not his.

If the social worker is disinclined to prepare for court, counsel may choose to proceed on that basis, and let the chips fall where they may. Alternatively, he may complete tasks that are properly part of the social worker's job, because he wants the case to succeed in court, but he still may not raise the issue of the working relationship directly. Counsel are generally reluctant to be seen to be "telling you what your job is" and instead, simply become less enthusiastic about working with you. Take the onus yourself to open communication lines to establish a consensus about what's working well and what's not. Adjustments may be necessary on both sides.

Most counsel have very specific expectations of the type of preparation for court that social workers need to complete, whether these expectations are spelled out or not. Find out what your counsel expects and tell him what you are prepared to do and what you are not. Tell your counsel what type of services you expect and ask him whether he is prepared to provide what you want.

Personalities enter into any working relationship, but these are rarely a problem if both parties are willing to state their needs and expectations and seek to accommodate each other with the goal of working well together in the common task of presenting the child's reality effectively in court.

When you encounter problems in working with your counsel, notice whether you are talking about your concerns with everyone but your counsel directly. There are few experiences more irritating to counsel than finding himself faulted for not meeting undisclosed expectations. You have an obligation to be clear about your expectations of counsel. Generally he will be delighted to hear directly what you expect of him, and pleased to pursue a discussion with you about what he can and can't do, along with the whys and wherefores.

It is worth observing that both you and your counsel could make your lives a whole lot easier if you got into a different line of work. Protection lawyers burn out for the same reason that protection social workers do. Lawyers who handle conveyances of land or who represent banks never seem to burn out. Be aware that your counsel is in protection work for the same reasons you are: the work is important, it is useful, and it involves assisting and protecting small citizens who may have no other protectors.

Take the time occasionally to give your counsel feedback for a job well done. Protection court process can be as frustrating to your counsel as it is to you. A willingness to give credit when due can serve to mitigate glitches in the working relationship. Your counsel is your best ally in the court process. You need to ensure that he sees you as his ally as well.

Lawyers are notorious for working long hours under severe time pressures. There are practical steps you can take to maintain mutual respect in the working relationship. Make appointments on time. Prepare for conferences. Give ample notice about problems that arise. Get advice early. Do what you say you will do. Deal with problems openly as they arise. In short, deal with your counsel as you would hope your parent-clients would deal with you.

HANDLING OF EXPERTS

Everyone's time is valuable. The time of experts has a meter attached, as a bill will be rendered. You seek to establish a cordial working relationship with the experts you have retained to testify in the case. Anything you can do to avoid wasting your experts' time is appreciated.

You need to be clear with experts about when written summaries of their opinions are required, and that the consequence of missing the deadlines may be that their evidence is inadmissible. You are entitled to instruct them as to what issues you want covered in their reports, and how specific you want them to be about the factual foundations of their opinions.

Court process involves a lot of waiting around since the duration of examination-in-chief and cross-examination is not very predictable. Ideally an expert witness should be scheduled so that she is the first witness called in the morning or afternoon, but this is not always possible. Where the expert is at court waiting to be called, she will appreciate comment during the breaks about how much waiting time will likely be required.

Trial dates often need to be changed and cases are frequently settled at the last minute, meaning that the testimony of the expert is no longer needed. The expert should be contacted immediately if the time for appearance is changed or if the expert no longer needs to come to court at all.

Sometimes agency counsel will be responsible for all dealings with the expert throughout. Alternatively, the social worker may have this liaison function, or the task may be shared between counsel and the social worker. Whatever arrangement applies in your own case, be clear about who is responsible for what in dealing with experts.

The impact of an expert's evidence in a protection case is difficult to predict. Judges will rarely decline to hear expert opinion, as there is wide judicial discretion as to the weight to be given to such evidence. Much depends upon the nature of the expertise proffered, the credibility of the particular expert, and the attitude of the particular judge. Because of these variables, and in light of the technical nature of much expert testimony, consult with your counsel on completion of the expert's evidence to obtain his views about the impact of the testimony.

COPING WITH FLUX

Litigation in other fields of law generally involves few surprises by the time the case goes to court. The focus is on what has occurred in the past and the court decision settles the matter in a final way, subject only to a possible appeal.

This is not so in the field of protection cases. Unlike other litigation, in which the pleadings are closed at some point, evidence of changes in the situation right up to and including the protection hearing date is admissible information. The family may move, parents may separate, siblings may move into or out of the home. Furthermore parental ambivalence about family problems does not disappear once the case goes to court. Parents may alter their position about your application several times in the course of the hearing.

Coping with flux can be difficult for the worker who develops a firm vision of how the case will proceed. Each intrusion of new developments will then pose an unnecessary strain.

Notice your attitude to the presence of new developments in the case.

Flux goes with the territory and presents the opportunity to alter strategy and create new solutions. The court case is best seen as proceeding step-by-step, just as your work with the family does outside of court. When new facts, new witnesses, and new positions of the parents are presented, consult with your counsel to determine whether you need to reconsider your own position on the case.

Chapter 9

BEFORE COURT:
HAT TRICKS, ZERO-SUM GAMES, WIN-WIN

SCAPEGOATING IN ACTION

A s the hearing date approaches, you may be aware of anxiety about
your performance in court. This is normal. Take care to notice your
emotional reactions and to share them with your colleagues. You are
entitled to feel whatever you feel. Simply expressing the emotion does
much to dissipate it.

If you find anxiety returning again and again, one technique for
resolving the fear is to acknowledge that it has nothing to do with the
present moment. Anxiety is fear about what may happen in the future.
When the events in the future arrive, you will do what you need to do.

Meanwhile your real choice is whether you are willing to focus on the
tasks at hand prior to the hearing, or whether you choose to use the
present moment to fret about the future. You need not judge yourself for
the choice you make, but you need to be aware of your choice.

It is easy for anxiety to transform itself into the scapegoating rituals
discussed in Chapter 1. Notice whether you utilize the period before the
hearing to find fault in the system and invest energy in the myths and
stereotypes about court process. If you find your thoughts running along
these lines, you need to take steps to reclaim your own power. Scapegoating
elements of the process is usually a device used to disown anxious
feelings. Acknowledging the anxiety removes the need to place blame.

Thorough preparation for the case, along with a willingness to pass
along the responsibility for the case decision to the court system, are the
most effective tools to put anxiety to rest. The corollary is that lack of
preparation aggravates anxious feelings. Sometimes the most straightforward technique for reducing anxiety is to focus on the preparation
tasks at hand. When you reach the point at which you feel intimately
familiar with the case and confident of your ability to articulate the facts,
anxiety tends to disappear on its own.

Scapegoating is gratuitous blaming motivated by a desire to disown responsibility. As the hearing date approaches you may notice not only your own tendency to revert to scapegoating elements of the legal system, but you may find yourself invited to assume the scapegoat role yourself at the invitation of opposing counsel or the parents. Simply become aware of what you are responsible for and what you are not, and decline to play scapegoating games.

ENEMIES AND ALLIES

The period before court is the most fertile time to create solutions for the case. The goal is to arrive at a solution to the protection issue which is satisfactory to both yourself and the parents. Whether negotiations bear fruit depends upon the attitudinal seeds which are sown by both sides during this period.

It is an error to assume a war room mentality as soon as the hearing date is set. This choice escalates the conflict and obliges opposing counsel and the parents to meet the stance with adversarial conduct of their own. The preferable attitude to take is that the court time is reserved and remains available if necessary, but that the immediate task at hand is to explore what solutions can be discovered in the common ground between yourself and the parents.

If opposing counsel and the parents take an adversarial stance from the outset, you are still at liberty to open discussions about possible solutions. The responses to these discussions will reveal a lot about whether the risk to the child is acknowledged and whether there is a real willingness to consider solutions to the family problems resulting in the intervention.

Sometimes an enemy mentality is unavoidable because there is no good will remaining. Your opposing counsel may be so versed in the adversarial mode that it is the only one she will consider. It is always worth proposing negotiations, but if things are too polarized you may need to abandon them early on and accept the inevitability of trial.

During negotiations you need to be clear about the nature of the problem as you see it and the minimum commitments required in any form of solution. You are ultimately an ally of the family, in the sense that you seek a solution that protects the child and hopefully reunites the family at the earliest point possible. Whether you are *seen* as an ally or an enemy depends a good deal on the style and tone you use to present your position and your concerns.

What you are aiming for here is a patent fairness and evenhandedness in your dealings with the parents and their counsel. It is tacitly understood that the advantages in the court process are all on your side. Parents do not live their lives with notebooks in hand, but you do. Most of the witnesses for your case will be professional notetakers like yourself, skilled in maintaining factual records of events. Parents may not have the resources to challenge your experts with experts of their own.

The trick is to convey firmness and clarity about your position without coming across as overconfident or oriented towards "winning" the case. The bottom line is that the family problems simply must be addressed. If there is a willingness to address them realistically, it becomes you to bend over backwards to present yourself as an ally in the search for a common solution.

SHARING THE EVIDENCE

Policy and practice vary widely as to how much of the evidence is shared with opposing counsel and the parents prior to trial. Because protection cases are normally dealt with summarily in lower court, parents are at a disadvantage as compared to litigants in superior court. Superior court litigation requires complete pretrial disclosure of evidence in hopes of narrowing the issues to be dealt with at trial and shortening the length of the trial itself. This discovery process includes the right to copies of all documents to be referred to at the trial.

Parents have few rights to pretrial disclosure of evidence in protection cases. Incongrously, parents involved in a traffic accident are entitled to far more disclosure of evidence than parents involved in a protection case. Except for prior notice of expert evidence, parents and their counsel do not necessarily find out the nature of the evidence in detail until the hearing. This factor tends to exacerbate the adversarial nature of the proceeding, unless you do something about it.

What you can do is instruct your counsel early on to provide opposing counsel with copies of the material reports and to advise what your position is, what the alternatives are, and what expectations need to be met. The primary reason for doing this is that it is only fair.

The secondary reason is that opposing counsel, without much concrete information about the case and perhaps with only limited instructions from his client, otherwise faces major hurdles in attempting to advise her clients about the true nature of the case, and in obtaining reasonable instructions about the real choices available to them. It is in *your* interest that opposing counsel be in a position to advise her clients about the strength of your case and the details about it, in hopes that the options realistically available can be discussed and produce a settlement. Without the details of the evidence, opposing counsel has no alternative but to proceed to the hearing.

TRANSCENDING THE ADVERSARIAL SYSTEM

Some agencies maintain a policy of requiring all negotiations to proceed between counsel once a hearing date is set or once parents have retained their own counsel. Others leave direct contact with opposing counsel at the discretion of the individual social worker.

If you have discretion in the matter, and subject to the advice of your own counsel, you need not hesitate to deal directly with opposing counsel to discuss your concerns and to hear the concerns of the parents. You should monitor the tone of these discussions to satisfy yourself that they are proceeding in good faith. If you develop a sense that opposing counsel really just wants to argue with you, you have the right as any client does to insist that communications go through your counsel only.

You should not negotiate with opposing counsel directly without alerting your own counsel. The agency position needs to be presented consistently and your case will be harmed if opposing counsel determines that you and your own counsel are inadvertently taking different positions.

The settlement conference is another vehicle for transcending the adversarial system. The conference may take place just between the two counsel, in which case you need to be extremely clear ahead of time in your instructions. It is your case, and your counsel needs to be instructed about what he is entitled to agree to on your behalf. In particular, he is not entitled to settle the case on his own, which would contravene his essential role as your representative. One technique to ensure difficulties are avoided is to instruct your counsel that whatever settlement terms are discussed are subject to your approval before the settlement is final, and that he is to tell opposing counsel that he will be meeting with you after the settlement conference to review the matter.

A settlement conference involving yourself and the parents as well as both counsel can often produce solutions. You may even want to include some of the witnesses who are in the best position to discuss the family problems face-to-face. The caution here is that you will not want the parents to feel outnumbered at the meeting.

With some families the settlement conference is the first time the family problems are truly confronted. With the court date hanging in the air and the presence of lawyers ready to proceed, the reality of the need to deal with things becomes apparent. There is no need to resolve everything at a single conference. If the nature and extent of the problem is acknowledged, the major hurdle to developing a solution has been overcome. Alternatives can be discussed, with a view to both sides thinking them over and renewing the discussion a day or two later.

Find out the way in which counsel involved are remunerated. Unlike yourself, counsel are generally paid on a case-by-case basis, or by terms of contract. If opposing counsel is sponsored by legal aid, find out whether she is remunerated for negotiation time. Legal aid programs which pay for court appearances, but not for negotiation, place opposing counsel in an awkward position.

You are being paid for your work, as is your counsel, but opposing counsel may have to do negotiation work for nothing. This does not necessarily mean that she will be unwilling to attend a settlement conference, but it does mean that you should go out of your way to ensure that the time is convenient for her, and that the time is not wasted.

Where cases are hotly contested and will require several days of hearing, some courts require pretrial conferences with the judge. The purpose is to determine readiness to proceed with the hearing and to see if the hearing time can be reduced by agreement at least on some of the issues. If you are not invited to be present for the pretrial conference itself, you might instruct your counsel that you intend to be close at hand so that you can respond to any proposals that come up.

There is little formality involved in devices that can be created to transcend the adversarial system. There are generally no "rules" about settlement conferences. Anything you can suggest which will tend to open up communication lines and increase the possibility that the substance of the problem is addressed will receive a hearing by counsel. After all, no one need be wedded to the notion of having a trial for its own sake. The goal is to protect the child, not merely to litigate. And all the players in the legal system know that solutions created out of court tend to work better than solutions imposed by the court.

INVENTING SOLUTIONS

The legal system operates with a zero-sum mentality. That is, one person's gain is at the expense of another person's loss, with no aggregate increase in whatever is at stake. Since lawyers are specifically trained to expect cases to be either won or lost, sometimes they find it difficult to suspend zero-sum tactics which have almost become second-nature to them.

To reach the zone of cooperation in which win-win solutions can be invented, you will likely need to navigate past a few power plays along the way. The quintessential power play is all-or-nothing: either you agree to return the child to the parents immediately, or you will have to go to court. Power plays which divert the communication process include interruptions ("I already know all that"), discrediting sources ("Everybody knows shrinks have the highest suicide rate"), redefinition of the problem ("If your agency did its job, we wouldn't be talking here today"), false logic ("I know lots of people who came from awful homes, who turned out just fine"), and passive power plays, such as ignoring ground rules, pretending to forget previous discussions, or ignoring refusals.

As discussed in Chapter 5, the task is to neutralize the power play without escalating or acquiescing. The steps involved are similar for all power plays: first, decline to make either-or choices, or to disown your position. Second, relax, so you don't get drawn into the power play game. Third, maintain a faith in the willingness of people to proceed cooperatively if they are offered the chance. Finally, discuss what the problem actually *is*, rather than argue about how it is being presented.

By demonstrating a willingness to ask for what you want and to listen to what the other side wants, you create a framework within which you and the other side can discuss possible ways of rearranging the factors to produce a mutually satisfying result.

The whole solution does not need to be created at once. Check out whether you are being heard when you state your goal of reuniting the family. "Mini-solutions," such as an extended visit, an offer of home-maker assistance or assistance with transport, or a willingness to map out a detailed plan in writing, can become building blocks for the general solution later on.

The test is whether the main energies are used to dispute facts and issues, or whether there is a willingness to invest in the greater energies required to use commitment and creativity to develop a cooperative solution. Once you have achieved cooperative common ground, solutions sometimes invent themselves.

LETTERS OF EXPECTATION

Upon obtaining an order that a child remain in your care for a period of time, the goal is to use that time to attempt to resolve family problems, such that the child can be returned. Some jurisdictions require the filing of a detailed case plan for the wardship period. If your jurisdiction does not, consider the use of a Letter of Expectations.

There is no magic formula for this device. The Letter of Expectations is a way of embodying your case plan for court use. The Letter of Expectations sets out the specific actions to be taken by the parents and by yourself during the term of an order of temporary wardship. The Letter should be dated, signed by the parents and yourself, and filed in court as an exhibit supporting your application.

For example, a portion of such a Letter might state that the parents agree to visit the child in the foster home three times per week, and that you will assist with arranging transportation for these visits. Or attendance at support groups or therapeutic programs can be specified. Some Letters specify a program of access visits in detail, moving from short supervised visits initially to overnight visits after specific milestones have been achieved.

In short, the Letter of Expectations is the place to nail down the concrete steps parents are prepared to make to manifest good intentions, and to declare the support services you are prepared to provide.

Acknowledgement of the dimensions of the family problems and agreement to a program to achieve reunion of the family are prerequisites to use of the device. As a result, the terms of most Letters of Expectation will be worked out in the context of applications which are unopposed or by consent. Some, however, will be used in the course of a contested hearing, if the parties decide to negotiate a settlement in lieu of proceeding with the hearing.

The use of this device is not mandatory; it just makes good sense. The parents want their child back and are entitled to know in the clearest possible terms what they need to do to achieve this result. You want to see concrete action taken on the problems at hand, and to be able to identify the level of agreement about what problems there are and what degree of commitment the parents are prepared to make to deal with them.

Lawyers and judges are great believers in paper. This is for a very good reason, namely that it is easy to argue about what happened and what was said, but much harder when the facts are put in black and white. The judge, having only those powers specified in your protection statute, is unlikely to have jurisdiction to impose the type of detailed terms you can include in a Letter of Expectations. His attitude to the document you create will be based on a test of whether the expectations are reasonable and practical. There is no point in having the parents sign a piece of paper agreeing to daily visits with the child if the prospect of this happening is obviously remote. There is no purpose to "setting up failure" on paper; the expectations need to be *achievable* by the parents.

A major benefit to you in terms of filing a Letter of Expectations in the court process is that if you later need to apply for a further order, the filed Letter will avoid a time-consuming disagreement in court between yourself and the parents as to what it was exactly that they were supposed to do. Instead of obliging the court to sort out what, if any, oral agreement existed between yourself and the parents, the judge can focus on measuring the concrete efforts of the parents to live up to their side of the written bargain since the previous court date.

The filed Letter need not be regarded as a permanent icon. During the term of the protection order, you can amend the Letter, delete terms, add terms, or make whatever changes by mutual agreement with the parents that will serve to reflect the current situation and intentions. Be prepared to file these amendments at a subsequent hearing.

Where parents have retained counsel, the Letter can serve to refocus the efforts of counsel. Some lawyers have a tendency to argue about whatever is in front of them. If nothing is on the table except for the type of order sought in your application, that's what the negotiation will focus on. But the court order is only the formal umbrella under which the details of real life occur. The Letter of Expectations deals with these details of real life events. Negotiation focused here will serve the case and the child in question.

The Letter of Expectations is not something you should attempt to put together the day before the hearing. Immediately after the initial intervention and removal of the child you should open discussions about expectations of the parents. Your own counsel needs to be apprised early of proposed terms, as does parents' counsel, if these parties are to have time to negotiate.

Simply put, energy invested in putting together a workable Letter of Expectations will often result in an unopposed application. A failure to utilize this tool, or some version of it, means that the case may end up being contested by default, as much as for any other reason.

STATEMENTS OF AGREED UPON FACTS

The use of "Statements of Agreed Upon Facts" can do much to reduce court time even in contested hearings and confine the focus of all concerned on the issues that are actually in dispute. There is no specific format or document required to file a Statement of Agreed Upon Facts. All the phrase means is that a set of undisputed facts has been reduced to writing, with a view to filing in court for the purpose of proving the facts stated. The Statement cannot be filed without the prior consent of opposing counsel.

The Statement can come to court in many forms. In some cases both counsel may agree to the filing of an expert's report as a Statement of Agreed Upon Facts, in the sense that the facts referred to in the report are accepted as accurate by both sides and the opinion itself is not seriously in dispute.

One or both counsel may wish to qualify acceptance of the report by specifying portions of it which are not consented to as proof in the case. If all parties are content to file such a report, it means that the witness will not need to be called to testify and opposing counsel forfeits her right to cross-examine the witness. A doctor's medical report is an example of a type of expert report which is often filed by consent without the calling of the witness. Of course, if any report contains disputed facts or opinions, the expert would need to be called, qualified as an expert, and examined and cross-examined in the usual way.

More mundane uses of the tool of preparing and filing Statements of Agreed Upon Facts include a statement of dates and addresses of a parent's various home addresses, a list of appointments made and missed, a child's attendance record at school, and a statement of access visits arranged and completed or missed.

The tool is useful where the evidence at stake is composed of a mass of nonvolatile detail on a single issue, and where these facts alleged are not seriously in dispute.

The actual content of the Statement will need to be "edited" to exclude those facts which *are* in dispute. For example, opposing counsel will not likely object to the filing of a statement giving a history of the times and durations of access visits, but she will object if the statement contains detail about the actual quality of such visits if this reflects poorly upon her client. These latter points are the proper subject matter of testimony, so that your version of the details can be tested by cross-examination.

To put it another way, if your point is that the quality of access was often poor, this point is not amenable to the use of a filed Statement— you will need to testify about it. But if your point is not as to the quality of the access visits, but merely the fact that there is a history of the parent arriving late or missing visits altogether, this point can readily be rendered in the form of a summary statement of what has happened.

Of course, you may simply get up on the stand to make the same point. If your concern is that the parent is so transient that this instability has affected care of the child, you can testify as best you can from memory as to the various places the parent has lived on various dates. But the more data on the issue, the more likely it is that minor errors of fact will be made and challenged, and an undue amount of court time will be spent to make the straightforward point. Be conscious of which parts of your case may be suitable for presentation in court through the use of this tool.

The protocol should be to type up a Statement of Facts for your counsel to submit to the opposing side. Opposing counsel may identify discrepancies with his client and amendments may be required before the Statement is in a form which both sides agree may be filed by consent. As the whole exercise is fruitless if opposing counsel will not consent to the filing of the Statement, avoid any references to facts or allegations which may be disputed, and which you can deal with by testifying directly.

Some opposing counsel will not agree to filing anything by consent, preferring not to lose the opportunity to attempt to trip you up over detail, so that the focus of the court process will shift somewhat from the point you want to make to the quality of your memory.

Like the Letter of Expectations, there is nothing mandatory about using this tool; it just makes sense. Its use will serve to "narrow the issues" in the contested hearing, so that nondisputed facts may be proven more quickly and easily and so that the court process can focus on the issues seriously in dispute between the parties.

ARMING OPPOSING COUNSEL

There are no fixed rules about how a social worker should deal with opposing counsel. Legal ethics forbid contact between a lawyer and another lawyer's client without prior consent of the client's counsel. So opposing counsel has no "right" to communicate with you directly any more than your counsel has a "right" to deal directly with parents who are represented.

If you are apprehensive about dealing directly with opposing counsel, or with a particular opposing counsel, you are at liberty to tell her to talk to your lawyer. There is nothing wrong with routing the information to be shared via your own counsel, and in some cases it is absolutely necessary. For example, your own counsel may wish to share sensitive information with the other side under cover of his own letter clarifying how the information can and cannot be used.

Consider the perspective of opposing counsel in deciding how to deal with her. One of the realities of protection cases is the advantage the agency has in terms of resources as compared to those of the parents in presenting their side of the case. Indeed, some opposing counsel argue that if the parents who are the subject of protection proceedings had the resources to fully, competently, readily, and completely put their cases to court, such abilities would likely be the very ones which would have enabled them to avoid an intervention in the first place.

The "typical" parent who is involved in protection proceedings is one who, for reasons that are not the subject of these materials, is unable to achieve control over his or her life, and who is so beset by personal pressures and traumas that he or she is simply unable or even unwilling to make the child a priority.

Consider, then, the likely content of instructions given by the parent to his or her counsel. These days dedicated parents virtually require full-scale diary systems and almost military logistical support to get Johnny to his soccer game, his dentist, his swimming lessons, and his paper route shack, let alone the additional appointments with teachers, parent associations, and sports organizations, not to mention possibly counsellors and tutors. The parent faced with protection proceedings, by definition, is not only unable to handle this level of organized parenting, but is also unable to assure minimal safety and well-being to the child.

The same factors which mitigate against adequate parenting skills mitigate against comprehensive instructions being given to parents' counsel. You may readily assume that from your point of view the whole picture is not readily disclosed, and that often instructions may consist of a terse direction to "get my kid back." Accordingly opposing counsel may be likely to focus primarily upon you and the supposed flaws of your case, all to be hammered out in court.

Given these probable realities of parent and opposing-lawyer perspective, make a conscious decision about what you wish your role with opposing counsel to be.

The first point is that keeping facts close to the chest simply plays into the adversarial component inherent in court process. This will be regarded by opposing counsel as playing hardball, and you have no basis for feeling surprised if you are treated in kind in court. But apart from this, nondisclosure is inconsistent with your role as representative of a protective agency. Conceptually, you have no vested interest in the result, in "winning cases." Your job in the court process is to provide the court with full disclosure and to acknowledge that the court is empowered to make its own decision on the basis of the facts and its own rules and procedures.

Consider the overall goals of the total process, and whether your proper duty may lie in *assisting* opposing counsel to do her job of representing the parents. If she has only the parents' information to go on, she is obliged to decide tactics for the case on that basis alone. If you provide her with full disclosure of the background and current information as well, this arms her with information which will affect the kind of advice she gives to the parents, and the kind of instructions she seeks from them about the case.

On this principle, you may wish to provide opposing counsel with your full case notes and all associated reports and background materials. You may further negotiate directly with opposing counsel, and meet with her and her clients to determine areas of consensus. Your counsel, of course, should be kept apprised of your decisions in this area. You may or may not wish to involve him in this process, based on your judgment about whether the involvement would be seen as an asset or an escalation by the particular parents and their counsel.

Do not embark upon this process unless you feel you can sustain the sufficient degree of openness. Your perception of events may not, in fact, be complete or accurate, and if you should become defensive or personally possessive of your own vision of events, the positions of all parties will simply harden.

It may help to step back occasionally and consciously monitor how useful you consider the negotiations to be. If the agenda turns out to be mainly pointing fingers and scapegoating you, you may decide to abandon the process and rely on the court process instead. However if you are evenhanded and reasonable, the direct negotiation process can result in concrete consensus and positive progress for the child, not to mention a consensual application instead of a contested trial. Part of the trick is not to be drawn into the dramas that may be offered, but to maintain the welfare of the child as your goal in all that occurs.

The extent to which you choose to develop skills in the matter of direct negotiation as an adjunct to the court process is a matter of professional choice. You are quite entitled, once the court process has been invoked, to mandate your counsel as the sole gatekeeper of information and negotiator on your behalf. But the *effect* of this policy decision on your part is that the court process will become more adversarial, in which case you should not be surprised at being dealt with rigorously on the stand. Opposing counsel can only use the tools available, and if you choose to discourage open dialogue, the tools remaining may involve an irritating harshness.

There are sometimes unreasonable, arrogant and insensitive opposing counsel. Some agency counsel, as well as some judges, may also be fairly characterized this way. There may even be occasional social workers who are generally regarded as displaying these qualities, though of course this would be a great rarity. Apart from these anomolies, the quality and nature of your dealings with opposing counsel have more to do with your own choices than any other factor. Arming her with the complete facts of the case ahead of time enables her to provide accurate advice to her clients and to seek appropriate instructions under the circumstances.

CO-OPTING THE COURT

Although the court has a legal mandate somewhat distinct from your agency mandate, the judge is essentially an ally in the common cause. He is also an ally of the parents, as the ultimate guardian of their legal rights to a fair and just proceeding.

There are beneficial elements to the judge's role that should not be overlooked in the search for the right way of presenting the real issues at stake in a protection case. Due to the nature of protection work, judges in family court play a more flexible role than is the case in most litigation.

In other litigation, for example, there is a tendency to get on with the trial and very sound reasons are required to justify requests for recesses or adjournments. Events break quickly in protection cases and most judges appreciate that it is in the interest of the child to interrupt the proceeding to permit settlement discussions at any point or otherwise to allow issues to be dealt with out of court. Do not hesitate to consult your counsel if solutions evolve in the course of the hearing.

There is also a quasi-parental role unique to a judge in protection court. Having heard innumerable protection cases, judges often have an uncanny ability to read between the lines as to the real issues going on in the family. A diplomatically-worded suggestion may result in the judge firmly telling the parent or the older child "the facts of life" regarding certain family difficulties, in hopes that such words from the authority of the bench may have a beneficial effect. No statute defines judicial jurisdiction to make such comments, but judges are prepared to exercise wide discretion if it appears useful.

Proceedings can be foreshortened by having the child speak with the judge in chambers, with or without counsel present. If the child is to testify, the judge will generally do most things requested to make the circumstances as nonstressful to the child as possible.

In short, the judge and the court process can have a therapeutic as well as a legal role in resolving family problems, although this aspect is not readily acknowledged. Consider what steps of this sort the court might take to assist in the case, and consult your counsel.

Chapter 10

IN COURT: SOCIAL WORKER ON TRIAL

EXAMINATION-IN-CHIEF

Most protection hearings, whether at the initial interim custody stage or later at the full hearing stage, are not particularly stressful. If performance in the new arena of the courtroom is unfamiliar, nervousness is to be expected, even in brief, unopposed applications. Occasional cases will be hotly contested and of these, some cases seem to involve so much pressure that the social worker is virtually invited to see herself, personally, as being on trial.

Hostile cross-examination is the aspect of court process which social workers tend to be most fearful about. The purpose of this chapter is to summarize the strategies for controlling emotional reactions while under the gun, and the tactics for reducing the likelihood of intense cross-examination in the first place. The test of whether you are coping with cross-examination successfully is whether you feel as if you are on trial yourself. If you do, you will need to invest energy in practicing the techniques which can protect you from experiencing the process this way. If you find you are already taking cross-examination in stride relatively comfortably, chances are you are applying these techniques already.

Your effectiveness in court depends much more on the court habits you make a policy of bringing to bear on *every* case, than on the rabbits you can pull out of the hat at the spur of the moment on the witness stand. This thesis applies particularly to the stress factor of court process. Although this chapter offers suggestions about steps you can take once you are called to the witness stand, the steps you have taken before the hearing takes place are even more important.

Brief mention is warranted of the two prehearing factors which have major impact upon the nature of your experience on the witness stand. The first is preparation. Weak preparation for the hearing aggravates every negative element involved in the court process. Thorough preparation muffles every negative element and eliminates many of them altogether.

The second factor is the making of a conscious decision about whether the particular case is likely to involve harsh cross-examination. This involves assessing the differential in convincing evidence to be presented by the agency side as compared to that available to the parents. Where there is serious disagreement about the facts and the parents provide opposing counsel with a detailed alternative version of events, the case will tend to focus on the evidence. Where the differential is too great, to the point that opposing counsel considers that she does not have an alternative version of events to present to the court, counsel may decide she is obliged to attack your credibility instead, as there is no other option. By comparing the relative strengths of the two sides of the case, you can make a conscious decision *before the hearing* as to whether the hearing is likely to involve challenges to your credibility. Forewarned is forearmed.

For most social workers, the first experience of testifying in court occurs just before or just after the intervention and removal of the child. The burden of proof in court is generally reduced at this stage, as compared to the later hearing. At the intervention stage you will generally be expected to show that there is "prima facie" ("at first glance," "on the face of it") evidence to support the apprehension; that is, that there was some apparent risk to the child, and that the apprehension was not arbitrary or capricious.

Some judges will make an order at the intervention stage based on reports filed alone, without requiring you to testify. If you are called to testify, don't merely read or cite the facts in your written report—the judge has already read them himself. Give the judge a verbal picture of what has happened, be clear about where the child fits in to the family constellation, tell him how long you've been involved with the family, and advise him of pertinent events since you wrote the report, and what your plan for the child is until the hearing date. Finally, advise the court of your position concerning access by the parents.

Your testimony at the intervention stage should usually take only a few minutes. Accordingly, you should be able to summarize the situation without notes and without many questions from your counsel. If you need to refer to your notes or have your counsel ask you questions to cover the ground, by all means do so. But since it is *your* case, it is reasonable for both the judge and your counsel to expect you to be intimately familiar with recent events, such that you can calmly relate them on the stand.

If you are unsure about what is relevant and what is irrelevant, get advice from your counsel. Stick to the facts; avoid opinions or the use of the jargon of your field. (Jargon from one profession is generally regarded with suspicion by another profession. Besides, it is clearly in the best interests of the child to relate clear sensory images of behavior and events rather than, say, refer to the child's "acting out" behaviour. Use of the terms of your trade invites quarrels about definitions and about your expertise in their use. The focus needs to be kept on the reality of the child's experiences, not on you.)

Your testimony is the court's first opportunity to assess how you regard your role, quite apart from the specifics of the case. Identify your own strengths and weaknesses on the stand. Observe your colleagues, and perhaps practice your testimony ahead of time. Be clear about what has happened, relate events clearly and chronologically, and be clear about what you wish from the court. The witness stand is the place to make your case, not prepare your case.

Consider asking your counsel for feedback about your performance at the intervention stage. If you are open to pointers, you will certainly get them. If you don't ask, your counsel will likely keep his mouth discreetly shut.

Your examination-in-chief is simply the series of questions put to you by your own counsel while you are on the witness stand. This may take only a few minutes at the intervention stage, or on subsequent unopposed applications or applications by consent, or it may take several hours in a complex, contested case.

Assuming an adequate Brief to Counsel (see Chap. 8), your examination in chief will flow from that. Keep in mind that your counsel can only *lead* you as to obvious formalities over which there is no dispute, such as prior legal proceedings and particulars of the parties. It is otherwise a rule of practice that questions in chief can give no hint within them of the answer sought.

You are entitled to refer to your running record if you need to refresh your memory, or if you have exhausted your memory. Although your right to refer to your notes is not normally challenged, opposing counsel is entitled to inspect your case notes and may also wish to determine that the notes were made relatively contemporaneously with the events to which they refer; later renderings of the story may not be referred to.

Your counsel should leave the matter of brevity or elaboration in your testimony to you; it is your case. Your testimony should be confined to your own personal observations or reciting admissions by the parties, although you will inevitably enter the realm of opinion when you describe the basis for the application and the plan you intend if the order sought is granted.

Previous comments distinguishing between testimony as to facts as opposed to opinion testimony apply to your general testimony here. Keep away from opinions ("she was drunk") rather than observations ("her speech was slurred, her eyes were bloodshot"), otherwise your lawyer will continually have to ask you what observations you made to arrive at the opinion, appearing thereby to be cross-examining you. Keep in mind the *"sensory image,"* the vivid word picture encapsulating an incident and a life story. The sensory images can take good hold in the mind of the judge.

Particularly where you are dealing with a long sad story, keep it chronological. The wealth of detail is hard enough for the court to absorb, without leaping about in time.

As a final question your lawyer should ask you if you would like to say anything further, in case he has missed anything. If he doesn't make a practice of concluding his questioning with this one, ask him to, at least with you. Then, if you want to elaborate, elaborate.

Notice the judge during your testimony. If the judge appears to be doodling rather than writing down your every word, wrap up the point and move on. If the judge interrupts your lawyer's sterling examination it may not be merely because he is bored with the line of questioning. Be alert for the possibility that some point is troubling him. His question may well give you a hint as to the direction the judicial wind is blowing. Pursue his line meticulously; who knows what fish has been hooked.

Some social workers, like some lawyers, have a penchant for battle and the smell of victory. Their demeanor bespeaks overconfidence and fairly demands they be taken down a notch. The better view is that protection cases are in essence nonadversarial and the role of the worker is likewise, to evenhandedly disclose all, whether it supports the agency or the parent.

By the time you reach the hearing stage trial there is merit to some detachment. The social work decision that brought you to trial has been made; the matter is now the responsibility of the court. Notice the shift in authority that occurs as you pass through the courtroom door. If you acknowledge it, your experience of testifying will be much more relaxed.

CROSS-EXAMINATION

The traditional rule for witnesses under cross-examination is to answer no more than the question asked. The corollary rule for counsel cross-examining is to ask only those questions for which the answer is already known.

Neither rule seems to have a lot of application to protection cases. For better or worse, opposing counsel rarely restrain themselves and more often than not you are given an opportunity to underline and elaborate upon your testimony in chief, digging the pit deeper. Sometimes it seems more realistic to say that if you haven't made your case by examination-in-chief, you still stand a good chance of making it by way of opposing counsel's cross-examination!

It is unpleasant to have your word questioned, still less in open court. Under attack, the best defense is complete sincerity. Opposing counsel sometimes have so little to go on that ruffling your feathers will suffice. Do not take refuge in condescension. The faintly superior hint of a smile, the patronizing tone of voice; neither of these become you as society's representative in the flesh. You are in court as an agent for the forces of good, but if you strut, you'll trip.

You have little or no control over the type of questions you are asked under cross-examination. But as Eleanor Roosevelt said in her autobiography, *This Is My Story,* "No one can make you feel inferior without your consent." The remaining sections of this chapter outline techniques you can use to retain choice and empowerment on the witness stand.

THE PERMEABLE BOUNDARY

The central key to combating emotional overreaction to stress on the witness stand is to maintain control of your personal boundary. Your personal boundary is the physical and psychological edge to your personal space. In the physical sense you will have noticed where this edge is located for you by observing how physically close you are able to allow people to stand before you feel uncomfortable.

Depending on cultural background and temperament, this edge varies widely from individual to individual. Everyone has had the experience of discomfort because someone is standing too close for comfort. For some, the discomfort arises at a distance of several feet; for others, no discomfort arises until the other person approaches within a few inches of the face.

The psychological boundary operates in the same way, but in terms of psychological, rather than physical, space. As with physical space, the outer edge of your psychological boundary is the point within which you feel invaded. Hostile cross-examination involves invasion of your psychological space. The hope is that you will make errors of judgment or self-expression in reaction to the sensation of feeling personally invaded. It is this same sensation which gives rise to the feeling that it is you, personally, who is on trial in the case.

You may find it useful to conceive of your personal boundary as analogous to the membrane of a living cell. The magic of the cell membrane is its ability to prevent harmful elements from entering the cell, while still allowing nurturing elements to pass through the membrane unimpeded. In the same way you can maintain control over your personal boundary on the witness stand, *choosing* to absorb and respond to those items relating directly to the child before the court, and allowing hostile items to dissipate their energies at the edge of your personal boundary instead of inside of you.

Developing awareness of your personal boundary involves noticing the choices available there. The simplest example is the choice available to respond to the content of the question being asked, without reacting to the tone of the questioner. As a witness in court you have a legal obligation to answer questions, but you have no obligation to absorb the negative packages in which the questions are sometimes delivered. One way of looking at the techniques described in this chapter is that they are all ways of maintaining choice at the edge of your personal boundary.

HONORING THE PROCESS

Take responsibility for any baggage you bring into court having to do with the myths and stereotypes described in Chapter 1. These are just ways of disowning the fear of taking the witness stand, by projecting the fear onto the other players in court. Choose to see the other players as having goals which are different from yours, but equally legitimate.

Notice whether you have made the choice to defer to the authority of the court once you walk through the courtroom door. From that point onward you remain responsible to discharge your *role* in the court process, but the responsibility for the case now belongs to the judge.

Notice whether you fully accept the role of opposing counsel to challenge and test the facts of the case. Your powers of empathy are of assistance here, particularly if you and a colleague have roleplayed the case from the point of view of opposing counsel. Questioning and testing the facts is the purpose of cross-examination. Where the facts are too unfavorable to the parents, their counsel may question and test *you,* and your qualifications, experience, and conduct. Getting defensive about such questions involves choice. You can also choose simply to honor counsel's right to ask what questions she pleases, and answer them.

Consider the elements of the court process which make you nervous to be analogous to going to the dentist. The overall rationale and objective of a visit to the dentist is sound and positive. By definition the visit may involve some pain, which dentists like to call discomfort. The intensity of the pain has little to do with what events actually occur, and everything to do with how much fear you bring with you to the dentist's chair. Flowing with the process renders it quite painless. If you resist, kicking and screaming every inch of the way, you only ensure that your pain receptors will operate with hypersensitivity.

By the time you reach the witness stand, your major work is already done. It only remains for you to tell your part in the story and allow the system to proceed as it will. Honoring this reality creates a sense of calm which helps you to play your part without violation of your personal boundary.

SPEAKING THE CASE

The perceived stresses of the courtroom can muffle awareness of the fundamental purpose of your being there at all. Ultimately, the process is not about burdening you with difficulty, or even about you at all. It is about the child. Your purpose is to speak his case.

Every act you take on the witness stand is measurable against this purpose. All else is secondary. You have special knowledge about the family, and special powers. You have had to intervene to protect the child, and you are simply in court to tell the story of what has happened.

There are a whole range of limitations on how you can present the case and a whole set of legal traditions in operation to test the veracity of your presentation, but it all comes down to telling the judge about the reality of the child's life experiences as you have observed them.

Incongrously, one technique for doing this effectively is to forget about all the other techniques for coping with court process, and to focus exclusively on telling the story. Ultimately, that's all you need to do, as best you can. If you can accomplish this, you will have done your job and served the child. It then remains to others to do what *they* are mandated to do. Speaking the case is the paramount task. The rest is secondary.

RESISTING INTIMIDATION

Encouraging a witness to choose to feel intimidated on the stand involves specific power plays, some of which are detailed in Chapter 4. If the power plays are successful, you end up feeling "less-than" your questioner. From that one-down position, answering questions clearly and confidently becomes a much greater burden.

If you choose to feel intimidated before you even get to the courtroom, you are relinquishing large parts of your personal power. You will need to take active steps to reclaim your power in order to be effective in court.

If you find yourself accepting invitations to feel intimidated by your questioner's manner, you may be misunderstanding the structure of power games. For a power play to succeed you must agree to play the game. Declining to be rushed, asking politely to finish your answer if you have been interrupted, answering repetitive questions patiently, and asking for clarification when you need it, are all techniques for refusing to play the game.

Counsel is entitled to ask you questions in a way which invites you to feel powerless, defensive, irritable, impatient, or confused. You are entitled to answer every single question calmly, fairly, and confidently, regardless of how it is asked. Receive the content of questions into your internal self, to consider your response. Watch for fancy packaging and when you see it, leave it just outside your personal boundary. Eat what you choose; choose what you eat.

MANAGING EYE CONTACT

Watch the judge and direct your answers to him. It is a curious social skill to direct answers other than to the person who is asking you questions. Accept responsibility to practice the technique if you find yourself habitually watching your questioner.

The issue is whether it is you who is in control of your own eye contact, or whether you have relinquished control to your questioner. The goal is to be able to make the choice yourself. If cross-examination is starting to make you feel a little tense, choose to look away from your questioner. Keeping your eye on opposing counsel splits your concentration. Do what makes you feel comfortable, but make sure that you are managing eye contact in a manner which ensures that questions receive your full concentration.

KEEPING THE FOCUS ON THE CHILD

All kinds of side issues arise in the course of a contested protection hearing. Blame, judgment, and denial are fertile forces which create multiple versions of the crisis events in a troubled family. Some of the questions about side issues are red herrings, pure and simple, having nothing whatever to do with the protection of the child. Some are related to the purpose of the protection hearing, but only just.

Most questions present the opportunity to respond in terms directly connected with the experience of the child. As an example, consider the question, "Wouldn't you agree that you could have made it a lot easier for the mother to see the child?" The question invites you to defend your conduct. The alternative choice is to frame the response in terms of the child's experience and needs: "It would be wonderful for Johnny to see his mother more often. He needs a lot of contact with his mom. We couldn't arrange as much contact as he needs because . . ."

Generalized, philosophical questions are best handled in the same way. If you are asked, "Don't you believe that kids are generally better off with their natural parents?" you can respond to the invitation to express a broad opinion if you wish. The other choice is to make the specific child real: "Johnny misses his mom a lot. He talks about his parents whenever I see him. If his mom and dad are successful in controlling the violence in the home so that Johnny is safe from it, he would certainly be better off at home."

The words you choose in replying to questions create a mental movie of the case in the minds of everyone in court. Choose words which ensure that the child is the hero in his own movie.

GIVING CREDIT WHERE DUE

One of your standard court habits should be to give all credit due to the parents at the beginning parts of your testimony. If you have adopted this technique as a regular part of your testifying in court, you will have spent a few minutes before court to decide specifically what good about the parents you can speak.

If you have forgotten to do this in the examination-in-chief by your own counsel, look for the opportunity to give credit when you are asked questions under cross-examination. There will be several places where you can acknowledge good intentions, at least.

Working with troubled families involves a lot of subjective judgment calls. Opposing counsel are sensitive to the possibility of bias, or to the possibility that you have taken a personal dislike to the parents. This issue is generally avoided entirely if your demeanor includes a willingness to take the initiative to give credit wherever possible. This also conveys to the court your professional understanding that you are not in court to "win" cases, but to provide the court with *all* the information about the family.

CONCEDING ERROR

You are a professional, doing the best you can. But you are not perfect and the court does not expect perfection. Opposing counsel will understandably focus on errors, particularly if your demeanor suggests a reluctance to admit mistakes or a desire to be seen as flawless under the glare of the witness stand.

When you are questioned about errors, notice the gravity of the error in relation to the whole picture of the family situation which has brought you to court. Minor errors should be conceded readily, particularly errors of memory concerning dates or times or places. You are not a computer.

Errors of judgment as seen through hindsight are more difficult to concede comfortably. Feel free to address the hindsight factor directly: "Yes, in retrospect a different decision might have worked out better. On the basis of what we knew then, it seemed the right decision. When problems developed, though, we took action promptly."

You are less likely to be asked many questions about minor errors if you are careful about expressing your certainty in response to earlier questions. If you are not certain about something, say so. If you don't know the answer, say so. A patent concern for accuracy in your answers will convey that you took care to avoid error wherever you could.

CLAIMING TIME AND SPACE

Opposing counsel is entitled to conduct her case as she sees fit and to ask questions as she pleases, subject to the discretion of the judge. Whatever style opposing counsel uses, you are entitled to claim the time and space you need to answer questions carefully and completely.

Some counsel attempt to build up a rapid rhythm to the questions which interferes with your ability to consider your answer clearly. You can choose your own rhythm for your answers by waiting a second or two before replying to questions. Court is not a game show and there is no need to hit the buzzer as fast as possible.

Most counsel ask questions from the counsel table. Some like to approach you on the witness stand, if the court permits. If you are uncomfortable with this, say so. "Would you please stand back a little? I feel uncomfortable when you stand so close."

If you are regularly interrupted without being able to complete your answer, your counsel will object. Your presentation is more effective, however, if you claim the right yourself to answer completely. "May I finish my answer before you go on?"

Long-winded, repetitive questioning can create strain and impatience. When opposing counsel uses this style, relax in the same way you might in dealing with a parent who speaks circuitously and has difficulty getting to the point. Embrace the situation with endless patience. Decide that you have all day if need be, and more.

REHEARSAL AND TESTING THE WATERS

In a sense examination-in-chief by your counsel is a rehearsal for cross-examination, during which many of the same issues will be reviewed. One of the tasks of opposing counsel is to develop a strategy about the weaknesses in your case. Consider preempting the strategy by addressing the weaknesses comprehensively during examination-in-chief. This steals the fire of opposing counsel, who is then likely to spend much less time on the area in cross-examination.

The other advantage of addressing the weak areas under questioning from your own counsel is that opposing counsel is then unable to attempt to leave the impression that perhaps you were hoping the issue would not be noticed and that, in fact, you are not inclined to be fully disclosive to the court.

Weaknesses in your case can become the ultimate basis for the court's decision. Consult your counsel ahead of time to arrive at a decision about how such issues will be addressed.

Prior contact with opposing counsel before court may provide some guidance about how cross-examination will be handled, but not always. Some counsel use radically different styles when outside of court. In your communications with opposing counsel before the hearing, notice whether you are asked hard questions about the areas of likely concern. If obvious issues are not pursued, counsel may be saving the hard questions for court. Consider what they are likely to be, and how you will answer.

You may find it helpful to prepare for cross-examination by selecting an area of the case which you think opposing counsel will focus on and asking a colleague or your own counsel to role-play the cross-examination with you. Testing the waters ahead of time gives you a notion of what to expect, and may also suggest ways of handling lines of questioning that you will not be able to come up with so readily under the pressure of the witness stand.

EMPOWERING FANTASIES

The psychological goal of preparing for a contested hearing is to ensure that concrete steps are taken to neutralize the threatening aspects of the court experience as much as possible. To the extent that testifying is seen as a stressful event, it will *be* stressful. Each of the individual elements of stress has the potential to result in relinquishing parts of your personal power and rendering you less effective in presenting the child's reality to the court.

One technique you might experiment with is to create a fantasy in which the judge and opposing counsel wear outlandish clothes or conduct themselves humorously. Such fantasies have the effect of removing the intimidating veneer of power and authority which is manifested in formal court decor and expensive, immaculate clothes.

The court process is merely another human system, inhabited by ordinary individuals with special training to perform the task at hand.

You will perform more effectively if you see your fellow-participants in the process as fully human, rather than as imbued with the mantle of stereotype and high drama. The king puts his pants on one leg at a time, as other men do. Fantasies enable the person to be seen, not just the crown.

Another technique to reduce stress is to devise a brief meditation or fantasy in which a place of complete safety and calm is visualized. As achieving a sense of peace and calm is the essence of meditations, many specific visualizations of mental sanctuary are available in literature on the subject.

Your own meditation need not be complicated, elaborate, or lengthy. It need only be analogous to the kinds of brief exercises actors often use just before going on stage. Consider creating your own personal fantasy place, and practicing retreating to it mentally. After a bit of practice you may find it easy to take a few minutes before court to visit your own fantasy, coming out of it with a sense of calm that allows you to focus on your tasks in court free of nagging distractions.

REACTING AND RESPONDING

One difference between reacting to events and responding to them lies in the length of time each choice takes. As discussed in detail in Chapter 4, "reacting" ("acting again, repeating") involves swallowing whole whatever is offered on the outside and replicating the stress factor inside. "Responding" ("answering, replying") involves acknowledging what is happening on the outside, allowing only the safe parts through your permeable boundary, and *taking the time* to choose your response.

The pace and pressure of court process operates as a continuous invitation to react. In effect, personal power is given over to the push of external circumstance, such that the experience of testifying becomes a matter of constantly trying to cope.

You are entitled to respond, and to respond *fully,* to every question you are asked in court. You are entitled to take the time you need to consider the content of a question free of its packaging, and to consider how to reply carefully and completely. *Take* the time you need. Opposing counsel can only invite you to react. It remains to you to make a choice between reacting or responding, every time.

MAINTAINING YOUR WARM

Some witnesses seek refuge from the stress of the witness stand in a stilted, formal manner. They are responsive to the questions, but they squelch the emotional content of their answers to the point that they seem mechanical.

For witnesses dealing with relatively dry, technical matters, the impact of a cold delivery may be irrelevant. As a social worker involved with the deeply human problems of children at risk, you need to present yourself in court as fully human.

This is just another way of inviting you to be yourself in court. Convey your natural warmth and caring. Smile pleasantly at court staff, the judge, counsel, and the parents. Representatives of large organizations such as the agency you work for always run the risk of being seen *as* the organization if no individual qualities are revealed.

Reveal them. *Enjoy* telling the positive sides of the story. *Use* eye contact to connect with the other people in the courtroom. *Move* your hands or your body to elaborate on your point or to demonstrate. *Express* your feelings about the harsher events in the case. *Convey* confidence about the validity of your involvement with the family and your hopes for a resolution. *Honor* both the charm of the child and his pain. In short, be *present* in the courtroom.

All the other factors aside, the most convincing social worker witness is the one who declines to make major distinctions between how she behaves outside court and how she behaves on the witness stand. Just be yourself.

Chapter 11

AFTER COURT: THE POSTMORTEM

COMING TO TERMS WITH DEFEAT

The judge has ruled against you. As far as you can see, your position that the child required protection was sound, your case was prepared, your testimony was convincing, and cross-examination appeared to do your case little harm. But the judge has ordered the child returned home to the parents.

Considerations of possible grounds of appeal aside, your acceptance of the court's unfavorable decision is the real test of whether you are comfortable with the power of the court to make the final decision. But no matter how accepting you are of the system's division of authority to make protection decisions, there is a sense of gloom that descends whenever you do not "succeed" in court. You have worked hard to achieve a certain result, and "failed." Social workers differ in their ability to take court defeat in stride, but few would claim to be completely unaffected by an unfavorable result. In part, the legal system guarantees a sense of loss, due to its orientation to resolving disputes by deciding in favor of one party or the other.

On the positive side, what are the reassurances to be drawn from a court decision to return the child? There are at least a few:

1. You retain the power to intervene again, if circumstances justify a further removal of the child. You have been unsuccessful in convincing the court that the original incident precipitating removal of the child was serious enough to put him at risk, but the child remains subject to your right to intervene in future. The case has ended, but your right to protect the child in the future has not.

2. Your case has received a full airing of the facts. Despite the result, the parents are now aware that you take the situation seriously. Most parents will respond by altering their conduct to some degree, even if they get the child back. This alone reduces the risk to the child.

3. The importance of the loss is a reflection of the seriousness of the precipitating incident and the type of order that you were seeking. Where the incident is found by the judge to have been a relatively minor or isolated event, the negative decision may be of less concern. Similarly, if you were seeking a relatively minor order, such as a short period of supervision, the loss does not mean that you cannot continue to maintain contact with the family to see that things are safe. And in either case, the parents are now on notice that you take the situation seriously and are prepared to take legal steps if necessary.

4. In neglect cases the negative decision may have turned on the specific incident that triggered the intervention. Long-standing neglect cases sometimes present this sort of difficulty. When the family has been providing marginal care for a long time, social workers tend to see the real risk as involving the accrued impact of a long history of inadequate care for the child, even though many of the individual incidents considered in isolation do not amount to sufficiently serious behavior to warrant intervention. In such cases the specific incident precipitating the intervention may be seen in just this way, such that the court finds that the child was not at risk at that moment. In practical terms, a further intervention is often required eventually, with the court then granting the order sought.

5. In abuse cases, particularly involving sexual abuse, the evidence about the incident is often difficult to obtain. The mistreatment of the child generally takes place in the privacy of the home, with no other witnesses present. The child's testimony may be ambiguous due to immaturity, age, or poor language skills. The child's subsequent behavior, as viewed by experts, is subject to differing interpretations. The only comfort in such cases, where the judge finds that there is insufficient evidence to establish the abuse but you remain convinced that it took place, is that the parents are on notice that you remain concerned. Additional evidence may justify a further intervention.

If the judge provides oral or written reasons explaining how he arrived at his decision, you will at least have some guidance about the extent to which the court saw the specific evidence differently than you did. There may be some hard truths involved in examining the court's reasons for judgment. The true story of events, for practical purposes, is that which the court finds to be true. To the extent that the court makes findings of fact which differ from your view of the case, it may be a matter of the quality of evidence submitted.

When the court decision goes against you, it is worthwhile to consider the ramifications in terms of your agency. In the event of subsequent injury to the child, an internal review of the case, and of your conduct, is very likely. Any lost case warrants your reviewing your own handling of it, to establish whether you truly did whatever you needed to do. Where subsequent injury is involved, consider consulting your professional association to find out what support is available if you should need it.

Subsequent injury or even death of a child is the most devastating event to cope with in the protection field. The example of the "Baby Joseph" case referred to at the beginning of Chapter 1 was such an event. Subsequent to the court ordering the child returned home, the infant drowned in the bathtub when the mother left him alone in order to answer the phone. Although the reason for the intervention was the failure of the baby to thrive in his parents' care and there was no evidence of other parental conduct which put the baby at risk, the death of the infant precipitated immediate concern to place the blame for events somewhere. In such a case, the line social worker is the obvious person to receive the brunt of the blame.

Such tragedies are rare, but they do occur. Neither the social services system nor the legal system can protect every child from harm. Because of the possibility of professional action against you if you should ever find yourself in such a situation, as well as the possibility of civil litigation alleging negligence, consult your professional association immediately and give serious consideration to retaining independent counsel.

COMING TO TERMS WITH SUCCESS

When the court grants the protection order you seek, you have "succeeded" in the win-lose model of the adversarial system. It is important that success be viewed in the larger context of your work.

1. Notice whether your demeanor with the parents alters inappropriately because of the court result. Any tone of presenting yourself as having been "right all along" will only impair your ability to

continue your necessary work with the family. Ego must be a non-issue.

2. The parents' experience of a contested hearing impairs your working relationship with them anyway. After the court decision, you need to take steps to attempt to rebuild sufficient goodwill that you can effectively assist the family. The focus should be on the concrete steps that need to be taken to result in a reunion of the family. There is no point to rehashing the trial or spending a lot of time in discussions with the parents about outstanding grievances that result from it. The decision has been made, and the family needs to be encouraged to get on with their lives.

3. Remain aware of the flexibility involved in protection legal process. The order you obtained is not written in stone. If access provisions need to be changed, or if such progress is made that the full term of the order is no longer required, a further application can be made to vary the order. You can discuss appropriate variations with the parents as warranted.

At the same time, make sure that you give yourself credit for being effective in court when you achieve the result you seek. The order you have obtained is protective of the child, which is the purpose of all your efforts. Other players and witnesses contributed to this result, but don't forget to honor your own contribution.

ADDING TO THE TOOLBAG

At some point soon after the completion of a hearing, set aside some time to review the proceeding with a little detachment. Each hearing presents the opportunity to add to the toolbag of skills you bring to the next one.

Notice your strengths in court. What parts of your testimony did you handle especially well? Are you aware of anything you could have done to improve these parts further? Is there anything you would have done differently? Updating your inventory of strong court skills increases confidence and enables you to identify skills which you can share with your colleagues.

Notice what went wrong in the hearing. Every case has glitches that are a little painful to recall. The tendency is to move on and to try not to think about them at all. Yet these are often the most valuable sources of learning. For one thing, they are solidly embedded in consciousness, the way humiliating or embarrassing life experiences often are. Make use of them. Determine consciously what steps you could have taken to avoid the errors. Why did the errors occur? Could you have seen them coming, or were you caught by surprise?

If you have prepared the inventory of court skills and court habits discussed in Chapter 4, now would be a good time to review your self-assessment. It is helpful to take the trouble to observe how your skills are expanding and improving. Checking out how you did in the skill areas of lesser confidence is equally useful. *Use* the period following a hearing to take the time to reassess the contents of your toolbag.

CONSIDERING AN APPEAL

An unfavorable result in court may mean you want to consider an appeal of the judge's decision.

The findings of fact are not appealable. It is the prerogative of the judge to decide whether a witness is credible or not, or whether an event took place or not, based on the evidence presented. Appeal courts are not intended as a forum for a second trial on the same facts. Appeals are largely conducted by affidavit and other documentary evidence, including the transcript of the original hearing. Appeal court judges consider that the trial judge, having the advantage of hearing witnesses in person, is in a far better position to determine the reliability of the evidence presented.

An appeal involves asserting that the trial judge made an error of law. This means that he interpreted the protection statute incorrectly or made mistakes in the admission of evidence or in following appropriate legal procedure. Sometimes minor errors of law are found in appeal court, but the appeal court judges nevertheless consider that they are too minor to affect the original decision. To justify an appeal in practical terms, the error of law needs to be significant enough to warrant the appeal court overturning the decision.

Apart from an appeal, most jurisdictions enable a different sort of challenge to the trial judge's decision, often called a "judicial review." The allegation here is not that the trial judge made an error in interpreting the law, but that he either exceeded his jurisdiction as a family court judge, or he failed to use the jurisdiction he was duty-bound to exercise. An example of the first situation might involve a judge making a type of order that is not actually provided for in the protection statute. Judges cannot invent orders as they please; they and their courts are "creatures of statute." An example of the second situation might be where a judge declines to hear certain evidence which, on review, he is found to have a legal obligation to hear.

Challenging the trial court's decision is a highly technical matter. Challenges are also subject to strict time limitations. Consult your counsel immediately after the hearing if you require an opinion as to whether there are grounds to take the matter to a higher court.

DEBRIEFING WITH COUNSEL

In short cases social workers often do not trouble to arrange a conference with counsel to discuss the hearing afterwards. Some social workers do not do this even after protracted, hotly contested hearings. Make a conscious decision about whether you want time with your counsel to review what took place at the hearing.

There are two aspects of a debriefing session with counsel that can be useful. One is to get feedback on your performance in court, as seen from your counsel's perspective. Most lawyers are delighted to discuss the finer points of your testimony on the stand and how you handled cross-examination, if you ask. If you don't ask, they will discreetly infer that you would just as soon not discuss it. To encourage frank feedback, consider starting off by referring to a glitch or two that you feel you did not handle well. By opening with actual problems in your court work, you will reassure your counsel that you are willing to discuss and learn from your mistakes and are not merely seeking a pat on the back.

The other item you can place on the agenda during a debriefing session is the ongoing working relationship between yourself and your counsel. How well did you work together on this case? Did the two of you omit any important evidence in your testimony? Was counsel's style of questioning one which assisted you in articulating the life situation of the child? What adjustments in style might help for the next case? Was the division of responsibility for the task of preparing for the case one that worked smoothly, or are there misunderstandings that are apparent and need to be cleared up.

Without a debriefing session, both you and your counsel are left to your separate impressions of what happened. Some of these impressions may be inaccurate and worth sorting out. The professional relationship between you is improved and deepened by both you and your counsel taking the opportunity to review the parameters of how well you work together. You should take the initiative to set up a debriefing session, as your counsel is unlikely to. This is not because of disinterest; counsel love to review hearings after the fact. But if you don't suggest a debriefing session yourself, he will assume you don't consider it worth the time.

Chapter 12

LEGAL NOTIONS: SHAKY FOUNDATIONS

THE DIVISION OF POWER: PARENTS, STATE, COURT

The institution of the family is protected by the broad legal rights of parents to raise their children as they see fit, within defined limits. As the family is regarded as the fundamental social unit, parents have private rights to decide how their children should be raised, what type of religious training they should receive, if any, how they should be educated, and how they should be disciplined. In a free society such individual rights are not tampered with lightly.

The legal rights of children, by contrast, are given far less direct attention in the law. Children cannot make legal contracts, consent to medical treatment, vote, marry, or live independently, except to the limited extent allowed by a variety of statutes. Certainly children do not have the legal right to the love of their parents, to be emotionally supported, or to review the decisions of their parents. Much legislation and litigation involves children, but always in terms of what various adults think best for them.

Protection statutes define the right of children to be raised in a manner that affords them at least minimally acceptable parenting and freedom from harm. Social services agencies are mandated to assist marginal families to cope with their difficulties, and to intervene on behalf of society as a whole in the event that a child is at risk if he stays at home. The courts are mandated to use the protection statute and the court process to ensure that intervention into private family life is warranted, and to impose protection for a child on behalf of society as a whole.

Private litigation involving children, such as custody disputes, is a contest about custody as between two private citizens, usually the parents. Protection litigation is a contest about custody as between the parents and the state. Social workers need to be alert to the conceptual difference between the two, and to steer clear of involvement in private custody disputes except to the extent that a court orders otherwise. For a social worker to "take sides" in a custody dispute is not only beyond the protection mandate, but also represents, and will be characterized as, unwarranted interference by the state in the affairs of private citizens.

LAW AS A "LIVING TREE"

This old chestnut, familiar to first year law students, refers to the fact that the law is organic in the manner in which it evolves to accommodate changes in society. Lawyers are often accused of hedging in their opinions. This is partly due to the fact that, contrary to popular belief, the nature of the law is such that yes or no answers are rarely possible; rules have exceptions, the exceptions have exceptions, and what the law "is" at any moment in time is subject to the latest amendments to legislation and the latest interpretations of the legislation by the courts.

What this means to protection social workers is that the law affecting abused and neglected children changes over time. Just as your own practice alters to reflect current agency policy, what was once legally required in a protection case may no longer be required later on; remedies once available may be replaced by new remedies and new obligations.

Most protection cases do not turn upon fine legal points, but rather upon the facts of the case. When you do encounter a thorny legal issue, however, be aware that your counsel's opinion on the issue is a result of the state of the law at that time. A new court decision dealing with the point the next day may render his opinion obsolete. This is the nature of dealing with constantly evolving legal principles.

STATUTES, PRECEDENTS, AND ADJECTIVE LAW

Historically, in predemocratic times, the law consisted of decisions rendered by the king's courts. The body of court decisions handed down over the centuries is referred to as "the common law." Lower courts were bound to determine legal rights and obligations in light of the decisions of higher courts dealing with the same issues. These case-by-case decisions, having the force of law, are referred to as "precedents."

With the election of democratic representatives, statute law became predominant. Legislative bodies everywhere, from the highest national seats of power to the lowest municipal council and administrative tribunal, generate laws and regulations in enormous abundance. In many situations legislation was passed specifically to right perceived wrongs as seen in previous decisions of the courts. Courts are bound to enforce statutes, so long lines of decisions on a subject can be nullified overnight by the passing of a statute dealing with the same point in a different way.

The courts retain the function of interpreting the meaning of provisions in a statute. The result of this is that at any point in time what a law "says" is a combination of the specific wording in the provision itself, and the current interpretations of that wording as determined by courts of law.

With respect to your protection statute, a major focus of court interpretation has been on the stated grounds for intervention to protect a child. As discussed earlier, these grounds are defined somewhat differently in every statute, as each jurisdiction struggles to create ground rules for intervention which balance the right of a child to be protected against the rights of parents to the privacy of their family life.

The statutory grounds of intervention are constantly broadened or limited by court decisions interpreting what the statute intends. For example, historically most jurisdictions have required that seriously harmful parental behaviors be weighed in the context of a child who is already born. With the dramatic increase in the birth of drug-addicted babies, many jurisdictions now permit intervention at birth based on parental treatment of the child while in the womb. In some jurisdictions, the protection statute has been amended to provide for the problem specifically. In others, the courts have interpreted the existing statute in a manner that extends the protection mandate.

In addition to protection statutes and the precedent decisions interpreting them, the "law" in a particular protection case also includes "adjective" law. This is the body of rules and procedures dealing with the admissibility of evidence and the procedural requirements of the given trial court, including local practice.

Your counsel is likely to maintain summaries of precedent decisions interpreting your protection statute, as well as an evidence code and other materials specifying local "adjective" law. These are likely to be readily available to you for review, upon request. The purpose of developing some familiarity with the applicable statutes, precedents, and adjective law in your jurisdiction is not to make you a "mini-lawyer." It is merely to enable you to be comfortable in dealing with the sometimes technical side of presenting protection cases to court, and to get full value from the advice of your counsel.

THE COURT'S STRUGGLE WITH PROTECTION CASES

As discussed at several points, the adversarial legal system operates with many disadvantages as the forum for making decisions about abused and neglected children. A protection case is unique to the legal system, in that there are really no winners or losers in the ordinary sense. The hearing is about the child, but he is not a formal party to the proceeding. The agency has no vested interest in winning the case. The case is *about* the child and his safety, not about the rights of parents. The legal contest, in a sense, is more akin to the investigative aspect of your own work, than it is to any other type of trial in the courts.

The purpose of a protection hearing, by definition, is to provide the minimum interference with the family that will result in the child remaining safe, while looking to the reunion of the family in the long run if at all possible. And by definition the child is not old enough to protect himself; hence the involvement of a variety of adults on behalf of the state and society as a whole.

The courts have taken three alternate approaches to the unusual problems presented in protection cases. Consider the following in the context of your own court, to get a sense of which way your judge tends to lean. It is unusual for the court to acknowledge directly which approach it is taking, so you will have to make your own assessment on the point.

One type of judge, particularly if he also hears criminal cases and is used to the stricter standards of proof and procedure applicable to criminal law, operates from the traditional adversarial model. Tight judicial reins are exercised to exclude hearsay information and to ensure that the formalities of legal process are complied with.

When you come before this type of judge, your tackle had better be completely in order, because you will be expected to conduct yourself fully within the realm of the objective facts you are able to prove in court. This judge will also tend to assume the mantle of traditional judicial neutrality, leaving it to the parties alone to present their cases as best they can.

At the other end of the spectrum, another type of judge will conduct a protection hearing much more in the nature of an inquiry, with rules of evidence and procedure relaxed in aid of getting at *all* the information about the child's situation. Such a judge will admit items of evidence that would clearly be inadmissible in a criminal trial, in order to be able to consider all the information available. He will rely on his ability to sort through the information and determine which is reliable and which is not, rather than preventing some information from being heard in the first place because of restrictive evidentiary rules.

When you appear before this type of judge, some caution is in order. Just because the judge maintains an "open door" policy to evidence does not mean he is assigning all the evidence equal weight. He may *listen* to virtually anything you have to say, but he will still base his decision on those parts of the evidence that he considers truly reliable according to the usual tests. It is an error to interpret judicial willingness to listen to anything as a foundation for becoming overconfident about the case. This type of judge will tend to take a rather active role in the proceedings, asking questions himself and interrupting to clarify points of concern to him in the course of examination-in-chief or cross-examination.

Many judges attempt to strike a balance between the two ends of the spectrum. They will keep an eye out to ensure that the rules of due process are complied with and that their decision is based on convincing proof of objective facts. But they will also maintain a flexible approach, seeking to do what seems best for the specific case. Child witnesses and parents will be treated with sensitivity and informality, and there is a concern that all parties have the opportunity to have their full say, even if what is said is not always evidence in any usual sense. Such judges intend that all parties are not only treated fairly, but *feel* that the court process has been entirely fair.

If you appear before a judge who seems to attempt to balance the formal requirements of the law with a flexible, more informal approach, you would do well to ask your counsel to help you define the specific parameters and expectations involved.

Trial judges in protection cases are permitted wide latitude in the manner in which they conduct their courts. Judges have broad discretion in running their courtrooms anyway, but in protection matters the variations are wider than in other litigation. The problem from your perspective is that judges are rarely called upon to spell out their view of the adjustments they make to ordinary court process in aid of protecting children. Notice the different judicial styles as you experience them, and take a moment to honor the silent struggle of judges to meet the responsibility of handling the most difficult type of case dealt with by the legal system.

REASONS FOR JUDGMENT

When the judge decides whether to support your application or to reject it, he may do so simply by pronouncing the order and leaving it at that. The great volume and similarity of many protection cases result in the vast majority of applications being dealt with without further comment.

When the hearing is contested or protracted, the judge will often "reserve" on the matter. This means he will take a short time, as little as a few minutes and as much as several days, to consider his decision. In these cases the judge will not only pronounce his order, but will also review the evidence presented and his findings about it by way of explaining how he arrived at the decision.

Sometimes the judge will announce his reasons for judgment orally, with all parties present. Other times the reasons for judgment will be typed up and read aloud in court, with written copies distributed afterwards.

Written reasons for judgment in protection cases are not nearly as widely circulated as reasons delivered from higher courts or reasons concerning other areas of law. This is unfortunate, in that a carefully reasoned judgment can assist other judges in other cases, but only if the judgment is collected and circulated.

Law reports are bound journals recording the written reasons for judgment in cases of particular interest, particularly the ones in which a new precedent is established. Protection cases are occasionally "reported" in various family law journals. Your counsel doubtless maintains files of reasons for judgment handed down by judges dealing with the protection statute in your jurisdiction.

You will find it useful to read a selection of judgments to get a sense of how the judge goes about his job. Reasons for judgment handed down in one of your own cases should be studied closely indeed. In lieu of the bald order alone, reasons for judgment will be explicit about which of the evidence the judge found convincing as well as which he did not. The judge's explanations of why certain evidence was persuasive or not will help attune you to the needs of the legal system. Specific findings of credibility and reliability of the various witnesses enable you to compare the judge's perception with your own. Well-written reasons for judgment present a unique opportunity to observe what hours or days of testimony boil down to in terms of their impact on the decision.

What is a Precedent?

A case referred to as a "precedent" is one in which (it is argued) the reasons for judgment of the court establish a legal principle of some sort which advances the interpretation of the law and which binds other courts to follow the principle established.

The majority of child protection applications, being unopposed, do not create precedents, as no reasons for judgment are offered giving detail as to how the court arrived at a decision. The court decision (an order) simply deals with the specific case, without providing guidance as to how like circumstances will be treated by a court.

Most reasons for judgment are not thought significant enough by the editors of the numerous law reports to "report" the decision for consumption by the legal community. An "unreported decision" is no less authoritative for its not having made it into the law reports, but as a practical matter, it is less likely that such a decision will be brought to the attention of the court in a new case if it has not been published anywhere.

Who Is Bound by a Precedent?

A lower court judge is bound by a precedent decision applying to the subject case if that decision is made by any superior level of court.

The lower court judge may consider a decision of another lower court judge, and may indeed treat it as a precedent decision and apply it to the subject case. However, a judge is equally free to (respectfully) differ with a fellow judge of like rank and make an alternative interpretation of the legal point. As a result there may be conflicting interpretations of the law which may render a legal issue unresolved until an appeal of the point is eventually taken to a higher court, which then resolves the issue.

A precedent decision is not binding in a subject case if counsel can convince the court that it may be "distinguished." For example, consider a precedent decision which establishes the principle of "anticipated deprivation" for a baby born drug-addicted. How broad is this principle? To how many other categories of anticipated deprivation might the principle apply? Would the decision suggest intervention in cases where the mother had smoked or drunk alcohol throughout the pregnancy? Counsel for the mother in such a case could be counted on to argue that the subject case should be "distinguished" from the precedent decision, and that the principle established should be confined specifically to cases of children born drug-addicted.

Over time precedent decisions may be "extended" to apply to related situations, or "confined" to the facts of the particular case. If you are involved in a case in which you feel a recent precedent decision is supportive, you and your counsel will need to give thought to whether the counsel for the parents may successfully distinguish the subject case from the precedent, such that the court finds that the precedent does not apply.

"Citing" Precedents

One example of a precedent decision establishing a principle of antici- pated deprivation is formally cited as follows:

Superintendent of Family and Child Service v. D.J.
28 R.F.L. (2d) 278, S.C.B.C. (Proudfoot, J.) 1982
(1984) 4 W.W.R. 272
(1982) 135 D.L.R. (3rd) 330

The formal name of the case is taken from the parties before the court. The confidentiality that surrounds protection proceedings results in initials being used to identify the parent involved. Law reports are referred to in a citation in standard abbreviated form. The first citation underneath the case name indicates that the reasons for judgment have been reported in the 28th volume of Reports of Family Law, second series, at page 278, that the decision was made by Madam Justice Proudfoot, and that the reasons for judgment were handed down in 1982.

The subsequent citations indicate that reasons were also published in Western Weekly Reports and Dominion Law Reports. A formal citation commonly lists all reports in which the reasons were published, to facilitate locating the judgment. So if you have a citation for a case of interest to you, you should be able to use the law reports in your local law library or courthouse to look up the reasons for judgment and examine the actual decision.

Often the judge writing reasons for judgment will refer to precedent cases he has considered in arriving at his decision. References to such cases are cited in the manner noted above, so you only need to find out from your counsel what law reports are referred to in the specific abbre- viations cited, and where you could have a look at them.

A Caution About "Headnotes"

The format used in law reports to publish reasons for judgment includes a few paragraphs at the beginning, in which the editor of the law reports attempts to summarize the facts of the case, the decision, and the legal principle applied. This summary is referred to as the "headnote" of the case.

Some law students and indeed lawyers attempt to get away with citing the phraseology of the headnote rather than quoting directly from the reasons for judgment. The implication is that they have not read the reasons for judgment, only the headnote. Most times the headnote gives an accurate precis, but it should be borne in mind that since headnotes are written by law report editors and not judges, headnotes do not bind anyone.

The point of caution here is that headnotes, and similar summaries of precedent decisions which your counsel may make available to you, should not be regarded as authorities in and of themselves. They are merely convenient references to the decisions of the court. Legal authority can only be found in the wording of the actual decision, the reasons for judgment.

The *"Ratio Decidendi"*

This term refers to the expression of the legal proposition established by a precedent case. It is the *"ratio"* of the case which binds other courts, and there may be argument about how the *ratio* should be most accurately expressed. As noted above, a headnote to a case attempts to express the legal proposition established, but you and your counsel must look to the decision itself to determine the principle established by the court.

"Obiter Dicta"

An *obiter dictum* is a statement made by a judge in the course of reasons for judgment which is not critical to the specific legal issues before the court. Hence *obiter dicta* have persuasive importance only, as indications of the thinking of the court, but as opposed to constituting part of the actual precedent which legally binds other courts to follow the same view.

An example occurs in the *D.J.* decision cited above, at pages 283 and

284 of the reasons for judgment. The lower court had made its decision on the basis of the original intervention report. This report referred to the child being "deprived of necessary care," one of various grounds specified in the subject protection statute. In the higher court reasons for judgment, the judge mentions that the lower court need not consider itself confined to considering only the original ground of intervention alleged, and that the agency is free to make its case on another ground, such as the child being "abused or neglected," if it chooses.

This kind of comment gives guidance to lower courts about the approach of the superior court to interpretation of the particular statute, but the comments are technically *"obiter,"* since the appeal grounds being considered by the higher court did not include making an issue of this particular point. If a legal issue is not formally before the court, judicial comments about the issue cannot form part of the *ratio* itself.

Higher court decisions in your jurisdiction will have modified, clarified, limited, or extended the provisions in your protection statute by interpreting the wording of statutory provisions. The portions of these decisions which form part of the *ratio* of the case are binding upon lower courts. The portions of these decisions which are *obiter* technically bind no one, although they are taken seriously for their persuasive value.

"Judicial Legislation"

Speaking broadly, the courts "make law" whenever they interpret statutes by establishing legal principles which are not contained in the statute explicitly. Your protection statute establishes the basic principles intended by your legislative body to be considered by the courts and your agency in the task of protecting children at risk. The courts "fill in the gaps" of the statute by determining how it should apply to concrete situations which are not specifically referred to in the statute itself.

It is clearly not possible for any legislative body to speak through the statute about how it wishes the courts to deal with every possible variation of a child protection case. So, armed with well-established legal principles relating to children generally, the courts extend, vary, modify, and limit the statute through precedent decisions on particular cases that arise under it.

This process is a logical and analytical one, although some argue that legislative bodies are mandated to make laws, and that the courts should confine themselves to literal and conservative interpretations of the statutes as they stand. Others support judges who seek to extend statutes to meet what they interpret to be the original intention of the legislators.

In any event, should the courts arrive at an interpretation of a statute which the legislative body considers is contrary to the policy it intended the statute to embody, the legislative body can always amend the statute accordingly and "reverse" the courts. Until the legislative body takes such a step, however, the current "state of the law" is composed of the statute *and* the precedent decisions interpreting it, both being subject to rules of evidence, practice, and procedure.

Precedents and Social Workers

Reviewing applicable precedents is a primary responsibility of your counsel. However, considering that a lower court judge can only make a decision based on a precedent if it is brought to his attention, you may consider it prudent to monitor precedent decisions as part of your casework.

If you have located a precedent which you feel may apply to one of your own cases, consider its applicability before or during consultation with your counsel by inquiring as follows:

1. Is the decision of a superior court or at the same level as your trial court?
2. Is the precedent point taken from the reasons for judgment, as opposed to the headnote or some other summary?
3. Is the precedent point taken from the actual *ratio* of the decision, or is it "merely" *obiter?*
4. In any event, is the precedent point directly applicable to the "case at bar" (the subject case), or are the legal issues in the case at bar distinguishable from the precedent you wish to cite?

THE HEARSAY RULE IN PROTECTION CASES

The evidentiary rule against hearsay is based upon the unreliability and unfairness that would be involved if legal decisions were based upon statements made by people who have not come to court to testify directly. Hearsay evidence is considered unreliable because, without the maker of the statement, there is no way to know if the statement is being accurately quoted, and there is no way to assess the credibility of the maker of the statement if he is not on the witness stand. It is also unfair to opposing counsel to admit a hearsay statement into evidence without her having the opportunity to test the truth of the statement by cross-examination.

The major exception to the rule against hearsay which is of paramount importance in protection cases concerns admissions by a party to a proceeding. The rationale for this exception is that statements made by the parties to third parties is more likely to be reliable, and in event the parties to a proceeding have the opportunity in court to explain, deny, or clarify previous statements as they see fit.

Parents are parties to a protection proceeding and statements made by them constitute a major portion of the agency case. Parents in protection cases are often obliged to recite their histories and explain events pertaining to the child to a wide variety of professionals, including doctors, nurses, police officers, day-care operators, financial assistance workers, alcohol counselors, and teachers. All such admissions are admissible by calling these witnesses to tell the court what the parents said.

The admissions made by the parents are also a proper factual foundation for the opinions of experts, who may not only interview the third parties but also obtain the reports and recordings which other professionals are accustomed to keep as part of their own work.

One way to foreshorten the court hearing and reduce the number of witnesses necessary to call is for you to present the admissions made by the parents to third parties to the parents directly, for response. You can then testify, not to the admission relayed to you by the third party (a hearsay statement), but to the response given you by the parents when you told them what they are alleged to have said (an admission of a party to the proceeding).

You should consider presenting third-party statements to the parents in any event, out of fairness. If you propose to make decisions on the basis of admissions apparently made by the parents to third parties, it is only fair to give the parents the opportunity to clarify and explain what they actually said and meant.

An evolving area of adjective law is the manner in which legislative bodies and the courts regard hearsay statements in protection cases in general, and in sexual abuse cases in particular. "Admissions" made by the child to a third party such as yourself are not ordinarily admissible since the child is, incongruously, not considered a formal party to the protection proceeding. The question is whether you, or a psychologist or other professional interviewer of the child, can quote what the child has said without the stress and trauma of the child having to testify in court.

Important court decisions have held that due to the special nature of protection proceedings, and the likelihood in many sexual abuse cases that the child's statements are the basis of the whole case, witnesses may quote what the child has said providing there are circumstantial assurances that the quotation is reliable and accurate. In addition, some statutes have been specifically amended to override the rule against hearsay in protection cases, or to broaden the admissibility of hearsay. Hearsay evidence is often critical in abuse cases. Consult with your counsel to find out the exact status of the rule against hearsay in your jurisdiction.

Chapter 13

JOURNEY TO PROTECTION:
HELPING YOURSELF, HELPING THE CASE, HELPING THE CHILD

MEETING YOUR OWN NEEDS

As a member of the helping professions, you have chosen a type of work that, ironically, often invites you to neglect your own needs. The pain and suffering around you are profound enough to make the stresses you are feeling yourself seem trivial by comparison. Perhaps, by doing just a little more, by extending yourself only a bit further, you can make it all right.

Maybe you can, maybe you can't. But at what cost?

The cost in the court process is the risk that you will not only hurt yourself if you don't make your own needs a priority, but you will also be less effective in court.

When you consider the impact of some of the battle-mentality elements built into a protection case, and add the demands of coping with court process to the already intense demands of the family in crisis, you are a good candidate for a sense of inadequacy at the very least. You need to take care of yourself, or you will have trouble helping to care for others.

What are the sorts of things you need emotionally in order to flow confidently through the process of presenting a protection case?

Acknowledgment

The nature of the system is that you are responsible for the case, but you only work in a vacuum if you choose. Ask for what you need. If you have given everything you have for a case, it helps to know that your efforts are noticed. If they aren't noticed, make them noticeable. Tell your supervisor about what you have accomplished. Share the results of your efforts with your colleagues.

179

It is not a matter of seeking praise. It is a matter of obtaining acknowledgement from those you work with that you are involved in a common cause. People don't necessarily know what you are doing unless you tell them. Talking about your work is a way of obtaining confirmations that your work matters, that you are doing your best, and that others are there for you if you need them. Keeping the good things secret can be as isolating as keeping the bad things secret. Draw strength from others. You are only as alone as you choose to be.

Ventilation

Protection cases can be emotional roller coasters. Events move rapidly and unpredictably. The legal process is built on the belief system of finding fault, assigning blame, and punishing. No matter how cooperative everyone is attempting to be, feelings of anger, pain, and fear go with the territory.

The danger is getting stuck in the negative emotions. Turn the feelings into words. Expressing the feelings does not solve the problem, but it releases much of the negative energies behind them.

You do not have to be reasonable about your feelings. They are just your feelings, and logic has nothing to do with it. You are entitled to experience all the anger, blame, or judgment that you feel. Just because you are prevented from releasing these negative feelings to the people who have triggered them does not mean you have to keep them to yourself.

Ventilation does not require the presence of the person who created the feeling. It is not a matter of where you put the feelings once they are released outside; the important thing is that they *get* outside. Speaking them out loud by yourself or with a trusted friend may work best for you. Some people achieve ventilation by writing their feelings out, or indirectly, by drawing or physical action. Discover the techniques that work best for you so that you remain up to date with yourself and so that you don't get in your own way.

Ventilation is completed (for that moment, anyway) when the negative feeling is sensed as already moving into memory and the past; it is no longer part of your living in the present moment. If part of the negativity remains in the moment, notice whether you censored any of the feelings you wanted to express. Feelings that are required to pass muster in order to be acceptable to be expressed, will not be expressed. If this is a problem, choose to set a later time to judge how nasty your feelings are; use the moment to honor your heart and *express* what you actually feel.

You are entitled to the emotional reactions you have to the frustrating parts of the process. But you need to ventilate, otherwise the bottled emotions will color the way you handle yourself and keep you off-center. To be effective in court you need to be acting from your center, not from left field.

Respecting

Your self-esteem from the work you do is connected with your respect for the work and your respect for yourself. Sometimes dealing with the legal system involves exposure to experiences that seem abrasive, rude, intrusive, insulting, or demeaning.

Polish your back with the wax of your own self-respect and let the irritants roll off. Treat these experiences the way you would if their source was an upset parent. They are offered for your consumption, but they are toxic. Decline to partake.

Self-respect is measured internally, not externally. The work you do has real importance. You are there for a good cause. If others choose to see you as less than who you are, that is their choice. It has little to do with you.

Limits

The system is designed to assign cases to you administratively. But the only one who knows your limits is you. When you are involved in a protracted battle in court, the last thing you need is additional responsibilities. Caseloads vary widely, but it is the supervisor who assigns the cases.

Consider refusing to accept a new cases until the court proceeding is completed. Tell your supervisor the reasons why you will be unable to undertake additional work. Explain the demands of the court case, and ask *her* for assistance.

Find out what kind of support your professional association offers concerning caseload policies. Decide whether you are there to do a job, or a good job. Doing a good job demands standing up for your right to do the job properly. Speak your limits; you may otherwise be imposed upon.

Complaints

Aspects of the case may turn out to bother you. Your counsel is not asking you questions in the manner you requested. A witness says something quite different on the witness stand than when you interviewed her before. A psychologist produces a late, or shoddy, report. Someone gives you bad advice.

The danger lies in keeping justiable complaints to yourself, where they fester. When they are spoken out loud, you can move beyond them. Choose to speak them without blaming or criticizing. Describe them in terms of their impact on you, not in terms of the flaws they reveal about others. Few people resent hearing concerns when the expressions of them are owned by the speaker, rather than laid upon the listener.

Some complaints, such as those about the judge, or opposing counsel, or the parents, are not appropriate to express to people directly. This does not mean you have to eat them, and leave it at that. Express them to a friend, colleague, or spouse. The important thing is to get them out, so that you are unburdened by bottled irritations. It takes energy to keep things inside. You can choose to reclaim this holding energy and use it for better things.

Expectations

"Success" has an out-of-the-ordinary meaning in the context of protection cases and families in crisis. Small gains need to be deliberately celebrated. Sometimes there are only small gains; sometimes no gains at all.

How you feel about the experience of presenting protection cases to court has much to do with your expectations. These need to be consciously chosen and defined. The problems that make your work necessary are not ones that you can solve alone. Protection cases that go awry are powerful vehicles to create a sense of disappointment to the point of making you wonder whether it's all worth it.

Maybe it isn't. It depends how big a charger you have chosen to ride, and how much of the world you are intent on helping. Noticing the impact of your own expectations is an important part of taking care of yourself in protection court work.

Keep an eye on the larger questions. Is the world a bit better off because of the work you do? Maybe not in this case or that, but overall, certainly. Are *you* better off for the work you have chosen? If you are taking care of yourself, you must be. Otherwise it may be time to move on.

LIMITATIONS OF THE JOB

The limitations of the social work job in court are painfully plain:

1. You will not be able to protect every child from neglect or injury.
2. You can encourage people to change, but people have to make their own choices.
3. If people are unreasonable before the hearing, odds are good that they will become more unreasonable as the hearing progresses.
4. Some lawyers will ask you personal or intrusive questions.
5. Some judges will be abrupt and impatient, or critical.
6. No one will save you from the rigors of court process. You have to save and protect yourself.
7. Some children will turn out to be worse off in your care than they were with their families.
8. Some parents may sue you if you make mistakes.
9. Elements of the legal system will not only appear to be insensitive and unfeeling at times, but they will *be* insensitive and unfeeling at times.
10. Some people will succeed in destroying themselves and their children no matter what you do. Some children who survive their families will repeat the cycle of abuse and neglect with their own families.

The list can seem endless if you let it. The point is that to be effective in protecting children in court, you need to look the limitations square in the eye. None of them diminish the great good that is done in individual cases, over and over again. But mistakes are made and none of the human systems is perfect. It is the imperfection that you need to make peace with, if you are to thrive in the work instead of merely coping. The wine glass is half-empty, but it is also half-full. Place your lips on the rim of the glass and *choose* which half you want to drink.

BECOMING AN ASSET TO THE CASE

Effective presentation of a protection case depends upon an exceedingly wide range of skills. Helping people in intense personal conflict draws upon your intuition and sensitivity. Translating your observations in court requires adaptation to the legal system's preference for objective description. Making the child's life real in the mind and heart of the judge calls for keen communication skills and the ability to create sensory images of the child's experiences. Assembling evidence, arranging experts, conferencing with counsel, negotiating with opposing counsel, and controlling the movement of data to the persons requiring it, all demand exemplary information skills.

However, the skills involved are identifiable and learnable. Most of the learning takes place on the job, and how much you learn is a choice over which you have sole responsibility. Taken as a whole, it may seem a formidable task. It is not. Everything breaks down into individual elements and choices. Do what you choose and choose what you do.

A social worker with good court skills is an asset to any case. Good court habits, brought to bear on every case, reduce the size of the task at hand. Most of the court skills and court habits you need are already in your professional toolbag of skills. It doesn't take much tinkering with the skills you already possess to allow them to serve you and help you serve the case.

The ability to balance the elements of the process, to see both sides, is always an asset. Can you see the bright side but speak your expectations firmly? Can you keep your eye on the goal but stay flexible? Can you retain your sense of humor but respect what is serious? Can you take advice but retain responsibility for your own decisions? Can you accept and express your feelings as you go along?

The legal processes involved can be complex, but each of the steps is simple, and ultimately human. The humanity that you bring to bear yourself is your best talent, one sorely needed by the legal system. You would not have entered social work unless you were a sensitive and caring individual. Whether you succeed in the court side of the job has a lot to do with bringing your sensitivity and caring along with you to court.

The technical skills of protection court work are there for the asking. The legal system is utterly obsessed with itself; its players love to share its mysteries. Lawyers and judges want you to participate fully in their arena, and to make it yours. Each of the players has a wealth of information about how the process works. Everyone loves to talk about his work, and everyone loves a listener. Treat the system as your asset and you become its asset.

While your best approach is to be real and personal, preparation counts. Doing your best with the parts of preparing the case that are your responsibility is all that is needed. Help with the thorny bits is close at hand. Players in the legal system tend to take their jobs and perhaps themselves very seriously. They are inclined to bend over backwards to assist those who approach life the same way. A solidly prepared case is a lawyer's delight. Do what you must to allow the delight to rub off on you.

OWNING YOUR POWER, SHARING YOUR POWER, GIVING IT AWAY

You are already empowered to be effective and confident in presenting protection cases to court. The same skills that you apply automatically in the field serve you in the forum of the courtroom. It is mainly a matter of noticing how they apply.

Perhaps the system should be set up so that thorough and careful training was available, or so that others would step in to protect you from irritating questions, or so that decisions about children didn't have to be made in an adversarial courtroom. But since the system doesn't work that way, you are far better off assuming the power to handle what needs to be handled on your own, and protecting yourself at the same time.

Notice your foundation premise about the court work you do. If your premise is that others will rescue you, protect you, make your decisions for you, and make things easier for you, you have given away most of your personal power. The person who is in the absolutely best position to make things easier for you, is you.

If you choose to be your own authority in your work, you will find it easier not to allow others to make your decisions for you. You can listen to the advice of your counsel and consider it, without automatically doing what you are advised to do. You can consider propositions from opposing counsel, and test their validity against your own judgment about what is needed. You can hear comments from the judge, and take them or leave them as you see fit. You are the authority for your case, and responsible for the decisions you make.

At the same time, you have a commitment to share your power once an intervention has taken place. The intervention is your decision, as is the type of order you are applying for and the plan for the case. You retain a lot of power in deciding what evidence you want your counsel to call and what terms of settlement you are willing to consider.

But once you walk through the courtroom door, you must not only be seen to acknowledge that the power to decide the child's fate is now shared with the court, you must also acknowledge the shift in power inside. Coming to terms with the right and duty of the court process to deal with protection cases is a matter of being willing to share control because you see yourself and your role in perspective.

You are still in the best position to keep the child in perspective in court. Sharing power with the legal system releases energy which you can use on the witness stand to ensure that the reality of the child's experience remains the focus of the proceeding.

Due to the nature of the legal system and the belief system underlying it, you will be exposed to countless invitations to give your power away. But the invitations are just invitations. Each one you accept is a choice. Each one you reject is a choice. How empowered you remain during the court process is precisely a question of how empowered you choose to be, nothing more. Power is not taken away, it is given away.

ACCEPTANCE AND FORGIVENESS

Protecting abused and neglected kids is painful work. The primal pain is the pain of the child, hurt in body, mind, or spirit. Close to that is that pain of being unable to guarantee love, of working within the limits of what the system can do. Then there are all the little points along the way through the court process where blood is drawn.

The temptation of righteous indignation is great. Cruelty to a child snaps the spine of human understanding; it is unforgiveable.

But forgive you must. To take on the pain, even to fuel judgment about a great wrong, only leaves you paralyzed. To forgive, you do not need to sanction the abuse or the abuser. You need not agree with the wrong or the wrongdoer. Forgiveness is about acknowledging what is and what has been. It is a way of releasing the self from the prison of self-righteousness. It is yourself you need to be able to forgive, not the other.

The pain of the work is endless, but the well of forgiveness is bottomless. Dump the pain there, or it will eat at you from the inside out.

Acceptance of what is enables you to proceed. Accept that parents are doing the best they can with what they have to work with, just as you are. Condemn the action, if you must, but forgive the person whenever you can, if you are to offer hope. You are the last resort of light to the children of darkness. Leave judgment to others and walk in sympathy, not vengeance.

Acceptance and forgiveness are tools to enable us to fully offer ourselves in the present moment. They are ways to release the past and uncover the possibilities of the present. When the legal system bites you in the hand unexpectedly, you are merely being summoned to awareness. Acceptance and forgiveness mean seeing what is, seeing how the system operates, letting it be, and letting it go. Take the awareness that comes with acceptance, and the release that comes with forgiveness. In so doing, you reclaim the moment for yourself.

EITHER-OR

The legal system is the quintessential belief system based upon either-or. That's okay.
You are the and.

LOVE IN PROCESS

The hurly-burly of too many cases and too little time makes it easy to lose sight of what you have chosen to offer to a fear-ridden world. Take a moment now and then to notice the engine of your efforts, which is love.

Notice love at work. Where you see steps toward the light, you offer praise. Where you see conflict, you offer solutions. Where you see pain, you offer healing. Where you see hopelessness, you offer choice.

In short, where you see fear, you offer love.

Society can dress up the process with all the courtrooms and rules and lawyers it wishes. It has all these in plentiful supply. Through your work you must swim through this process, but you are not of it. You are not a spoke in the wheel of the law, nor its axle. You are the one who gives it hard push in the direction of love, and hopes for the best.

Every time you speak your heart for a child at risk, you add a little bit of light in the world. If, along the way, bits and pieces of the world rub up against you with anger and distrust, so be it. It takes more than a lawyer or two to diminish the good that you do. Master all the courtroom skills and strategies you wish; they will stand you in good stead. But what it all comes down to in the end is that you are an agent of love, not law, and love is a far more powerful force for justice than the law will ever be.

Off to court with you, now. Tell the judge what love can do.

INDEX

A

Adjective law, 167
Affidavit, 96, 161
Appeal, 122, 161–161
Attorney (*see* Counsel)

B

Brief to counsel (*see* Counsel, agency)
Burden of proof, 121–122, 144, 168
Burnout, 13

C

Case conference, 91–92, 123–124
Case notes
    admissibility of, court, 96
    hearsay in, 94
    identifying provable facts in, 92–95, 118–119
    jargon in, 94
    opinion in, 94, 146
    refreshing memory from, 145
Child
    access visits to, 84–85
    best interests of, 76, 83
    drug addiction of, 167
    intervention (*see* Intervention to remove child)
    return of, to parent (*see* Parent)
    rights of, 165
    risk to, 34, 37–38
    safety of, 34, 168
    speaking with the judge in chambers, 142
    statements of, 114–115, 158, 176–177
Common law, 166
Counsel, agency
    briefing, 16–17, 39, 116–121

consulting with, 117, 124–126, 154
    debriefing with, 162–163
    instructing, 46
    myths about role of, 7–8
Counsel, opposing
    myths about role of, 7–8
    negotiating with, 130–132, 134–135
    perspective of, 139–141
    settlement conference with, 132–133
    sharing evidence with, 131–132
Court
    first appearance in
        burden of proof during, 144, 168
        expectations of social worker during, 79
        presenting the report at, 37–39
        purpose of, 45
    hearing in
        purpose of, 45
        serving notices prior to, 79–80
        stages of, 80–83
    role of, 104
    written report for, 45
Court clerk, 107
Court recorder, 107
Courtroom, 10–11, 107
Cross-examination
    defined, 48
    eye contact during, 65, 69, 150–151
    hostile, coping with, 7, 50, 54, 67–70, 143–144
    interruptions during, 64, 153
    leading questions during, 48, 63, 96
    pace during, 64
    repetitive questions during, 64, 153
    techniques of, 63–66
Custody
    child-oriented arrangements of, 25–26
    private disputes concerning, 165–166

D

Discipline, physical, 35, 112, 165

E

Evidence
    audio tapes, 97
    categorizing of, 113
    documentary, 96–97
    opinion, 81, 94, 146
    oral, 95–96
    photographs, 97–98, 114, 119
    real, 98, 114, 119
    video tapes, 97
Expert
    briefing counsel regarding, 120
    consulting with counsel regarding, 102
    costs of, 102
    challenges to, 101
    evidence of, general rule for, 98–99
    handling of, 126–127
    notice of, to opposing counsel, 131
    opinions of, 99–100
    qualification of, 101
    reluctance of, 102
    reports of, 100–101, 123–124
    social worker as, 81–83
Examination-in-chief
    at first appearance, 144–145
    at hearing, 145–147
    defined, 47–48, 96
Eye contact (*see* Cross-examination)

H

Hearing (*see* Court, hearing in)
Hearsay, rule against
    acceptance of, 68–69
    defined, 48
    exception to, 49, 176–177
    rationale for, 175–176
    use of, in case notes, 94

I

Interim hearing (*see* Court, first appearance in)
Intervention to remove child

assessing need for, 33–37
disclosure to parent of, 36–37
identifying abuse issues after, 112–114
identifying neglect issues after, 111–112
proof of facts of, 113–116
subsequent to hearing, 157

J

Joinder, 76
Judge
    myths about, 8–10
    role of, 104–105, 167–169

L

Lawyer (*see* Counsel)
Letters of Expectation, 135–137

M

Media, 30–31

O

Oath, consequences of being sworn under, 95
Obiter Dicta, 173–174
Opposing counsel (*see* Counsel, opposing)

P

Parent's counsel (*see* Counsel, opposing)
Parent
    admissions of, 114
    avoiding surprise to, 41
    giving credit to, 67–68, 152
    maintaining trust with, 40
    return of child to, 68, 75–76, 168
    serving notices to, 79–80
Parenting
    cliches about, 22
    minimal standards of, 36, 76, 83, 112, 165
Physical discipline (*see* Discipline, physical)
Poverty, 110
Power plays
    before court, 60–63
    in court, 63–66
Precedents, 171–175

R

Ratio Decidendi, 173
Reacting/Responding, 10, 57, 148, 155
Reasons for judgment, 108, 170
Removal of child (*see* Intervention)
Responding (*see* Reacting/Responding)

S

Scapegoat Syndrome, 5, 17–19, 129
Sexual abuse, 21, 24, 27, 30, 78, 92, 97, 114–115
Sheriff, 107
Social worker
    accountability of, 78, 103
    court skills, self-assessment of, 53–57,
        160–161
    credibility of, 16, 59, 67, 68
    discretion of, 77, 103
    fairness of, 67
    intimidation of, 61–62, 150
    intuition of, 15, 34, 89–90, 184
    investigation by, 35, 45, 78
    language of, 46, 47
    myths about, 15–17
    personal boundary of, 50, 147–148
    preparation by, 66, 106, 129, 185
    removal of child by (*see* Intervention)
    role of
        as firefighter, 27
        as rescuer, 41–44
        as witness, 67

    as expert, 81–83
    limitations to, 183
services offered by, 34
    testimony of (*see* Testifying)
State, mandate of, 35, 83
Statement of agreed upon facts, 121, 137–138
Statutes, protection
    historical origin of, 166–167
    interpretation of, 171–175
    language in, 33
    overview of, 75–77
Submissions, 108

T

Testifying (*see also* Cross-examination)
    anxiety before, 46
    avoiding hearsay while, 90
    avoiding jargon while, 68–69, 106
    conceding error while, 67–68, 143–156
    preparing for, 46
    role-playing before, 72, 153–154
Transcript, 107

W

Witnesses
    admissions of parents to, 115
    presence in court of, 107–108
    summarizing evidence of, 115–116,
        119
    subpoenas for, 120